Lines on the Water

Lines on the Water

A FISHERMAN'S LIFE
ON THE MIRAMICHI

David Adams Richards

Doubleday Canada Limited

Canadian Cataloguing in Publication Data

Richards, David Adams, 1950–

Lines on the water: a fisherman's life on the Miramichi

ISBN 0-385-25696-5 (hardcover); ISBN 0-385-25850-X (paper)

1. Fishing—New Brunswick—Miramichi River. 2. Salmon fishing—New Brunswick—Miramichi River. 3. Fishers—New Brunswick—Miramichi River. 4. Miramichi River (N.B.). I. Title

SH572.N4R52 1998 799.1'2'0971521 C97-931894-7

Cover photographs by Eric Colquhoun

Brook trout illustration © Alan James Robinson 1993

Miramichi map by Robbie Cooke-Voteary

Text design by Heidy Lawrance Associates

Printed and bound in the USA

Published in Canada by

Doubleday Canada Limited

105 Bond Street

Toronto, Ontario

M5B 1Y3

BVG 10 9 8 7 6 5 4 3 2 1

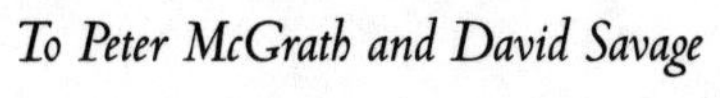

To Peter McGrath and David Savage

Acknowledgements

Thanks to my editor, Maya Mavjee, and my agent, Jan Whitford. And, as always, my wife, Peg, and children, John Thomas and Anton.

I love my river. I can tell you that. Each year there are days when the Miramichi shows its greatness—its true greatness—once again. And each year on the river, once or twice, I will meet men and women with a fire of generosity in them, of love for others that God required old prophets to have.

Mother Miramichi
Northwest Miramichi River
Little Southwest River
Newcastle
Miramichi City
Red Bank
Quarryville
Renous River
Blackville
New Brunswick
Juniper
Southwest Miramichi River
Doaktown
Boisetown
Cain's River
QUEBEC
NEWFOUNDLAND
NEW BRUNSWICK
NOVA SCOTIA

AS A BOY, I DREAMED OF fishing before I went, and went fishing before I caught anything, and knew fishermen before I became one. As a child, I dreamed of finding remarkable fish so close to me that they would be easy to catch. And no one, in my dreams, had ever found these fish before me.

I remember the water as dark and clear at the same time—and by clear I suppose I mean clean. Sometimes it looked like gold or copper, and at dusk the eddies splashed silver-toned, and babbled like all the musical instruments of the world. I still think of it this way now, years later.

As a child I had the idea that trout were golden, or green, in deep pools hidden away under the moss of a riverbank. And that some day I would walk in the right direction, take all the right paths to the river and find them there.

In fact, trout, I learned, were far more textured and a better colour than just golds and greens. They were the colour of nature itself—as naturally outfitted in their coat of thin slime as God could manage. They were hidden around bends and in the deep shaded pools of my youth.

I had the impression from those Mother Goose stories that all fish could talk. I still do.

My first fishing foray was along the bank of a small brook to the northwest of Newcastle, on the Miramichi. A sparkling old brook that Lord Beaverbrook took his name from.

My older brother and a friend took me along with them, on a cool blowy day. We had small cane rods and old manual reels, with hooks and sinkers and worms, the kind all kids used. The kind my wife used as a child on the Bartibog River thirteen miles downriver from my town of Newcastle, and her brothers used also, at the same time that I was trudging with my brother.

It was a Saturday in May of 1955 and I was not yet five years of age. Fishing even then could take me out of myself, far away from the worry of my life, such as it was, and into another life, better and more complete.

We had packed a lunch and had got to the brook about ten in the morning. Just as we entered the woods, I saw the brook, which seemed to be no deeper in places than my shoe. In we went (a certain distance) until the sounds of the town below us were left behind.

Leaning across the brook was a maple, with its branches dipping into the water. At the upper end of the tree, the current swept about a boulder, and gently tailed away into a deep pocket about a foot from the branches. The place was shaded, and sunlight filtered through the trees on the water beyond us. The boys were in a hurry and moved on to that place where all the fish *really* are. And I lagged behind. I was never any good at keeping up, having a lame left side, so most of the time my older brother made auxiliary rules for me—rules that by and large excluded me.

"You can fish there," he said.

I nodded. "Where?"

"There, see. Look—right there. Water. Fish. Go at her. We'll be back."

I nodded.

I sat down on the moss and looked about, and could see that my brother and his friend were going away from me. I was alone. So I took out my sandwich and ate it. (It was in one pocket, my worms were in the other. My brother doled the worms out to me a few at a time.)

I was not supposed to be, from our mother's instructions, alone.

"For Mary in heaven's sake, don't leave your little brother alone in those woods." I could hear her words.

I could also hear my brother and our friend moving away, and leaving me where I was. In this little place we were out of sight of one another after about twenty feet.

I had not yet learned to tie my sneakers; they had been tied for me by my brother in a hurry, for the second time, at the railway track, and here again they were loose. So I took them off. And then I rolled up my pants.

I had four worms in my pocket. They smelled of the dark earth near my grandmother's back garden where they had come from, and all worms smell of earth, and therefore all earth smells of trout.

I spiked a worm on my small hook the best I could. I had a plug-shot sinker about six inches up my line, which my father had squeezed for me the night before. But my line was kinked and old, and probably half-rotted, from years laid away.

I grabbed the rod in one hand, the line in the other, and tossed it at the boulder. It hit the boulder and slid underneath the water. I could see it roll one time on the pebbled bottom, and then it was lost to my sight under the brown cool current. The sun was at my back splaying down through the trees. I was standing on the mossy bank. There was a young twisted maple on my right.

Almost immediately I felt a tug on the line. Suddenly it all came to me—this is what fish do—this was their age-old secret.

The line tightened, the old rod bent, and a trout—the first trout of my life—came splashing and rolling to the top of the water. It was a trout about eight inches long, with a plump belly.

"I got it," I whispered. "I got it. I got it."

But no one heard me: "I got it, I got it."

For one moment I looked at the trout, and the trout looked at me. It seemed to be telling me something. I wasn't sure what. It is something I have been trying to hear ever since.

When I lifted it over the bank, and around the maple, it spit the hook, but it was safe in my possession a foot or two from the water.

For a moment no one came, and I was left to stare at it. The worm had changed colour in the water. The trout was wet and it had the most beautiful glimmering orange speckles I ever saw. It reminded me, or was to remind me as I got older, of spring, of Easter Sunday, of the smell of snow being warmed away by the sun.

My brother's friend came back. He looked at it, amazed that I had actually caught something. Picking up a stick, and hunching over it he shouted, "Get out of the way—I'll kill it."

And he slammed the stick down beside it. The stick missed the fish, hit a leafed branch of that maple that the fish was lying across, and catapulted the trout back into the brook.

I looked at him, he looked at me.

"Ya lost him," he said.

My brother came up, yelling, "Did you get a fish?"

"He lost him," my brother's friend said, standing.

"Oh ya lost him," my brother said, half derisively, and I think a little happily.

I fished fanatically for the time remaining, positive that this was an easy thing to do. But nothing else tugged at my line. And as the day wore on I became less enthusiastic.

We went home a couple of hours later. The sun glanced off the steel railway tracks, and I walked back over the ties in my bare feet because I had lost my sneakers. My socks were stuffed into my pockets. The air now smelled of steely soot and bark, and the town's houses stretched below the ball fields.

The houses in our town were for the most part the homes

of working men. The war was over, and it was the age of the baby boomers, of which I was one. Old pictures in front of those houses, faded with time, show seven or eight children, all smiling curiously at the camera. And I reflect that we baby boomers, born after a war that left so many dead, were much like the salmon spawn born near the brown streams and great river. We were born to reaffirm life and the destiny of the human race.

When we got home, my brother showed his trout to my mother, and my mother looked at me.

"Didn't you get anything, dear?"

"I caught a trout—a large trout. It—it—I—"

"Ya lost him, Davy boy," my brother said, slapping me on the back.

"Oh well," my mother said. "That's all right, there will always be a next time."

And that was the start of my fishing life.

That was long ago, when fishing was innocent and benevolent. I have learned since that I would have to argue my way through life—that I was going to become a person who could never leave to rest the *idea* of why things were the way they were. And fishing was to become part of this idea, just as hunting was. Why would the fish take one day, and not the next? What was the reason for someone's confidence one year, and their lack of it the next season, when conditions seemed to be exactly the same?

Or the great waters—the south branch of the Sevogle that flows into the main Sevogle, that flows into the Norwest Miramichi, itself a tributary of the great river. What infinite source propelled each separate individual fish to return on those days, at that moment, when my Copper Killer, or Green Butt Butterfly—or anyone else's— was skirting the pool at exactly the right angle at that same moment, and *when* was it all announced and inscribed in the heavens—as insignificant as it is—as foreordained.

When I was seven we moved to a different side of town where we fished a different stream. Here grass fires burned in the April sun. Here the sky was destined to meet the horizon beyond the pulp fields and tracks, where the woods stretched away towards the hinterland of the north, arteried by small dark-wood roads for pulp trucks. Boys not much older than I would leave school to work cutting pulpwood, or try to make money any way they could to help their families.

When we lived in the centre of town, we might have been described as city dwellers. But here we had different friends, far more ambitious and competent woods travellers. We were closer to the main Miramichi River. We would jump ice floes in the spring, with kitchen forks tied to sticks, spearing the tommie cod under the ice, as the sun melted these floes beneath our feet. Or we would wait along the side of the bank and throw hooks baited with carpet lint at the smelts that ran close to shore.

I grew up with poor boys who knew when the smelt run was on, and when the tommie cod came, because much more than me, they needed these things for their families to eat. We were wasteful—they were not. To them, fishing, and their fathers' hunting, had a whole different perspective. Some I grew up with ate more deer meat than beef, and relied upon it. And when they went fishing, it was less a sport than part of their diets. I remember a child who fell off an ice floe and started crying, not because he fell in, but because he'd lost the tommie cod he had promised his mom he would bring home.

As we started off to fish in June, the year I was eight, I did not know that out in that great river was the next generation of salmon moving up. They travelled in waves and waves of fish —perhaps seven to ten feet under the water and no more then fifty or sixty yards from the shore—absolutely unconcerned with me, or the fact that I would be fishing their descendants in the years to come; that they were the ancestors of fish I would some day see rise for my fly on the Renous or Little Souwest; that they were the progeny of fish that had moved up these rivers in the time of Caesar and Hannibal—the glacier fish (as David Carroll calls them), the salmon.

By late May to late June we would be fishing in the cool brooks and streams beyond town. We would sometimes jump a freight train leaving the Newcastle station, and ride it about a mile, as far as the Mill Cove turn.

I was with my brother and two of our friends, one who had the nomenclature Killer, and that morning we had walked down to the Mill Cove brook past the ancient crooked bridge, past the turn where the headless nun (a seventeenth-century French nun) would sometimes appear to unsuspecting lovers (almost always nearing the moment of climax) to ask them if they would be so kind as to help her find her head, which was chopped off by the Micmac, so that she could go back to France and rest in peace.

We passed the Cove, splendid in the early sunshine, where a small boy we knew had drowned the year before, in a neat little shirt and tie he had worn for a Sunday outing—when they found him, there were still sinkers and hooks in his shirt pocket. Then crossing the bridge, we turned to our left and went up the rocky brook.

The brooks we fished always had the same make-up. They were two to three feet deep, maybe four in the hidden pools, and sometimes no more than five to eight feet wide. They meandered and babbled through a green windy valley towards the great Miramichi, overgrown with alders and tangled with blow downs, which crossed them haphazardly, and for the most part the paths to and from them were paths made by children.

All during our youth we invented ourselves as cavemen, as Neanderthals. We had our own spots, caves along the side of the embankment, places on the streams that allowed us the luxury of this. This part of the spirit can never die if you are going to be self-reliant. If you think it can, try to excise it away from children, from one generation to the next.

Each year of our early youth we revisited spots on this Mill Cove stream that were rich with the memories of the year before. The dreams of children are poignant because they are so easily dashed.

That day, long ago now, we had gone to the left bank. It was hard going all the way. Many times we'd have to crawl through alders and thickets to get to a spot. Or cross the windfalls from one side to the other. And the spot where we were going was not much more than a small rip in the texture of the stream, about four feet long, just beneath the bank that we were walking on. Yet out of these small tiny pockets in this most unassuming remote northern stream came wonderful trout—ten inches long and more—which to boys of eight and nine years old were God-given.

There were four trout taken that day. It was a warm day and we were walking back and forth on the windfalls that crossed the brook, wearing sneakers and short-sleeved shirts. It was almost time to go when we decided to cross, once more, a windfall to the right because there was a pocket further down the brook that Jimmy remembered, which we hadn't been to yet.

"It's right over there. I caught a trout there last year this same time," he yelled.

We put our rods in one hand and started to cross the windfall that was angled higher on the right bank than the left. Jimmy went across first and then my brother, then Terry, and then me. I am fairly clumsy and have fallen in many times. When I hear of old river guides on the Miramichi who've done handstands going down through the rapids in a canoe, I can only say I've unintentionally done that as well.

I started inching along the windfall and glanced up to see the rest of the boys already on the other side and moving along the bank. The water babbled swiftly beneath me. I took one more step, and then another, and suddenly found myself under the windfall I had been crossing, and underwater as well.

The log was directly above me and I couldn't stand up. There was a rock in front of me so I couldn't go ahead, and one of the tree limbs from the windfall was preventing me from going backwards. Even when I lifted my head I couldn't clear the water.

I just had to hold my breath and watch the boys walk away. I was literally between a rock and a hard place and I must have looked something like a trout. I can tell you there was no panic. But I sure thought I was in a bad spot. With the sound the brook made, the boys had no idea I had fallen in.

But then Terry said something to me, and when I didn't answer he turned. I wasn't on the log, but he could see something under it.

They ran back and hauled me out. They were all quite pleased they had saved my life. So was I.

The pool Jimmy wanted to fish was half full of sand and silt. The year had changed it, and aged it forever. That's why he hadn't initially found it.

We went home. It was June 1959.

This was the day of the Escuminac disaster, when men drifting nets for salmon got caught in a storm as fierce as any seen at sea. Their boats were twenty-five feet long, the waves they faced were eighty feet tall. But so many of them would not leave other boats in trouble, and continued to circle back for friends being swallowed up, cutting their nets so their drifters wouldn't sink, but being swept away, tying their sons to masts before losing their own lives. Handing lifelines to friends instead of keeping them for themselves. If this sounds heroic, it was. It was.

That night I slept through the death of thirty-five men out in the bay.

Just after this experience, I went with my brother to dig worms in an old garden. We were going downriver to fish on the Church River, which we did every summer, until I was about eleven, with our father. My brother took the pitchfork and started to dig, while I shook the sod and picked up the worms. I happened to drop a piece of nice plump sod over my left foot. I stood there counting up the three or four worms we had managed to capture.

"This looks like a good place here," my brother said, and he drove the pitchfork into the sod above my foot. I looked down at it, in a peculiar way, I suppose, and then he jumped on his pitchfork to get some depth.

And then he lifted the fork, and me, and my foot up with it. One of the tines had gone right through the top of my foot, and I landed about four yards away.

Mr. Simms, the man who came to our aid, and carried

me to the doctors, and who'd known about my near-death experience in the Mill Cove made the observation: "Fishing's pretty darn hard on you, Davy, isn't it."

I suppose those were the truest words about me he ever spoke.

Two

FOR ALMOST A MONTH after this I was laid up, and moved about with the aid of crutches. Which made me think of myself as a Randolph Scott movie character, and had people being very nice to me.

I see old pictures of me at that time now and realize how tiny I was for eight. I might have passed for five, with my left arm almost useless. Yet something in me must have been determined—for I was climbing cliffs, jumping ice floes and freight trains, getting into fights with boys my age. As a matter of fact, I never thought of myself in any way except willing to give most things a shot.

In the year 1900, when my paternal grandmother was about seven years of age, there would be so many salmon moving up the main Miramichi in June that people wouldn't be able to sleep at night because of the splashing these great fish made moving upriver. People who lived upriver, ancestors of people I know, would fish by night with lanterns in their hands.

All that is changed now, but I have sat out and watched salmon break water all those clear white nights of July and August near my cottage and at different camps of friends along the river—especially if there was a holding pool near a brook. Newcastle was much different then. It graced its people with more of the natural world and less of the manufactured one. But it had the nefarious cauldron of political bigotry well ingrained in it.

My grandmother, an Irish woman, came from Injun town—her father had come over as a young boy after the potato famine in Ireland. The Orangemen used to parade through the Irish settlement for a number of years, on July lst. And my great-grandfather used to dress in his suit and lie in bed, certain he was about to be murdered, and preparing for his wake as best he could.

The river was much cleaner, the salmon more plentiful, the long logs and pulp logs that would be boomed after the great river drives, where the timber cut on faraway river branches and streams would be floated out to the town mills.

All of this is gone now, gone forever. Eighteen-wheelers carry the pulp and hardwood along arteries of roads, and those roads are travelled by fishermen and hunters who would have had little access to those faraway pools a generation or two ago.

There were more salmon and trout then, and biologists and conservationists have been telling us since the commercial fishery of the sixties that things must change in order for the great fish to continue. When I see nets strung out across our river, or listen to the tales of certain poachers, I realize there are many hard lessons ahead of us, and that our children or our grandchildren will some day pay the price we were unwilling to pay.

The manufactured world has done more for us, and less for the salmon, than anything I know. The politics are more polite, but like all politics, vulgarity rests just under the surface. And it is this political environment and this manufactured urban world that has set out to distribute salmon as if you would wealth or property. It will not be, and can't be done.

On my mother's side of the family they were all woodsmen, and went to work when they were children. They were and are strong-willed and independent people, with a mixture of self-reliance and old-time Presbyterian ethics. When I was a very little boy, about 1954, my uncle Richard Adams (my mother's brother), who already had a reputation as a great fishing guide for the rich Canadian and American sportsmen, brought a salmon home to my grandmother on the old homestead above the Matapedia.

I remember that fish—lying on an old newspaper in the kitchen, with a bit of blood along its gills. I imagine the fish weighed almost as much, or perhaps more, than I did. And I remember also how deftly my grandmother took a knife and opened it up, and the scales that looked like bits of silver in my hand.

My uncle picked me up and carried me down the hill towards the deep-green Matapedia River where he had moored his canoe, and set me in it. It was a long Restigouche canoe, much bigger than the Norwest Miramichi canoes. He wore work boots and green work pants, though the day was very warm, and he turned and walked away from me, towards the bow.

I was hoping to go fishing. This, however, was not the case. We were not going to go fishing at that moment. Someone wanted a picture, and I was the object for this picture. Far over our heads the CN train trestle glimmered in the sun. The picture was taken—it was laid away somewhere to be forgotten. And my duty fulfilled, I was picked up and carried back up the hill to the porch. Off in the cool kitchen the salmon lay. It had come out of a pool that morning. My grandmother had cleaned it, and had taken the gills from it, and scraped most of its scales off.

The salmon was taken by my uncle on a Black Dose, which is the fly he loves. He had started to guide when he was twelve years old, and was far more comfortable in the woods than out of them.

"I will catch a fish some day," I said, looking up at my grandmother and then looking at the huge bright Atlantic salmon, with its glassy dark eyes and just the start of a bill, that had known worlds that are secret to us all.

"Oh, those Miramichi salmon—they aren't like our Matapedia salmon," my grandmother said, teasing.

I grew up in an area of fishing rivers and fishing life without getting to go very often. Sometimes I would pass over a bridge over that dark rum-coloured water, or notice it in the distance as we went on our way somewhere. Sometimes, city bred (or town bred) as I was, I would have to listen to the trials of the adventurers who had gone out into that mysterious physical world. And sometimes I would seek these adventurers out.

So when I was twelve, I visited at times with Mr. Simms, who lived next door. As I sat on his porch in the August shade, with the soft smell of the mill far away, he often told me of the fishing summers he and his brother had when they were boys.

"We fished all summer from an old patched-up canoe that never handled well. We ran the Norwest Miramichi every other day—the loop from the Miner's Bridge down to Wayerton, and every time we went we caught fish. We hit the sea trout run, and the salmon run, and the grilse run, and all summer long, poling downriver around every bend, we never saw another soul fishing. The river was deserted back then, can you imagine? Imagine that great salmon river being deserted? No one was much interested in the flies I tied back then—the Royal Coachman, the beautiful Dusty Miller, the Cosseboom.

"There were people who fly-fished of course, but none of the young lads I knew bothered. The rods were a lot heavier than they are now. We had old rods, one a them was my father's twelve-foot rod, and he never used it but he won it on a raffle."

He showed me his diary—most of it written a decade or more before I was born.

I took a fish today from Dr. Wilson's, his diary read. *Cool and cloudy, water just right, after dinner wind come up.*

His diary was old—so you were talking of old fish,

generations ago. Winters that covered up those pools and turns on the river, in a deep bed of indolent white sleep, and springs that came and opened those rivers once more, with the ferocious crack heard for miles. When thousands of tons of salmon moved through our tributaries, where small rocks and eddies were remembered as "the hot spot" in a pool for a few years before the pool changed. When the sounds of men's voices changed with time, and the sound of different canoes coming around the bend changed, and the fly patterns changed too—they became more accommodating to the fish perhaps, or more utilitarian.

And it was a generation ago when Mr. Simms showed me his diary. And an old cane rod that was splintered with years of use now forgotten about—the moment of ballet and battle on a cloudy day around a corner somewhere far away, when he was not much more than a boy. Yet, in some sadness, I relate a million fish have come and gone since then, and bears have crossed those rivers in silence, and moose have fed in the lily ponds, and salmon have jumped the sea lice off, in the splendid dusk coming into a pool, with no one in the world to see.

When I was twelve or thirteen, and since my father didn't fish salmon, and my uncles who did were all on the Matapedia some 250 miles away in the big woods of Quebec, I was at a loss over how to go about learning.

I wanted to fish and hunt. Being able to use only one arm didn't deter me. I just had to learn to compensate. I've been good at doing that.

I didn't start off fishing salmon. Not many do. Perhaps those lucky individuals who are born very close to the salmon pools can recount taking fish at six years of age. But I was not able to do that.

So when I was young, we went down to Burnt Church, which was so named because General Wolfe on his way to Quebec fired a volley at the French Catholic church standing on Micmac ground and hit it. The wharf has the sea smell of salt and saltwater fish, and of course what I always associate with wharves near the sea—dried-out seaweed and tar.

Sometimes on drowsy days, I would walk up to the Church River, alone, past the great cow pastures of downriver farmers, fishing for trout, in the little darkish pink pools, and looking for—and being somewhat wantonly cruel to—frogs.

If it was August, I would get nothing but chub on a hook, and spend the day looking at the clouds moving haphazardly across the sky, already tinged with the feelings of fall. And now and again I would see some leaf seared by an early cold draught of air. On other days, for more excitement, I would walk to the wharf during the changing of the tide and fish for perch and eels, in the black tossing water of the Miramichi Bay.

The perch were wonderful to fish with chopped-up pieces of discarded meat I got as bait from the general store.

The eels were great fighters too, and since I never ate them (I had eel soup once, and once I had some eel in paella in Spain), I would take them off the spin hook and toss them back in. Some of them seemed as big as pythons to me then.

Eels don't die until sundown. That is when their body stops moving. It may be an old wives' tale but I've witnessed it a number of times. If I happened to be fishing beside someone who kept his eels, I had to move my position because I couldn't stand to watch them all day long, writhing and twisting and wanting to get back into the water, and not understanding why I couldn't help them. I couldn't tell the man to put his eels back because he was going to have them for dinner, so I would have to go down to the far end of the barnacle-strewn wharf to fish alone.

At the far end of the wharf I seemed to be staring out towards a water-filled world alone. The waves here were darker and colder, the breeze sharper. Far away I could see the point of Portage Island.

One hot day when I was fishing there, I decided to jump

in off a tying pole and swim to the ladder about twenty feet away. I had seen my brother and his friends do it. And I felt it couldn't be that much trouble.

The swells were wonderful, the water was very green and deep, and because of the salt the sun dried you very quickly.

Off the end of the wharf there had been mackerel moving all day—you could see their silver bodies about ten feet beneath the surface, charging along. They are wonderful fish, mackerel are, as wonderful (almost) to fight as a grilse. But I couldn't catch one that day. I would try to touch them when I dove in, and I would come up to the surface, feeling exhilarated.

But once I felt something swimming beside me as I came up. I turned towards the ladder, and this huge head popped up and stared at me. It was a seal. He calmly looked at me, blinked, barked, and lay back on his shoulders to eat a mackerel. He was about three feet away, and he must have thought that I was probably fishing like he was, and he wanted to brag to me about how it was done.

Once or twice a summer I would get out with the drifters, jigging mackerel. These were small boats, twenty-eight to thirty-four feet long, that drifted at night for salmon. During the off-season or during the day, some fishermen would rent them out for tours or mackerel fishing.

This was when I was between the ages of ten to thirteen. We would start off in the morning, but never seemed to make it anywhere until after lunch. The small open lobster boats were painted white, had small wheelhouses (sometimes not a wheelhouse—the wheel being open on the starboard side—but it had a tiny forward cutty, which always had the peculiar scent of soiled blankets, wine, and oil). It must have been a hard and at times lonely existence for some of the men who lived along the coastal shores.

We would have two or three lines down off the side of the boat, fishing off the far side of Portage Island, which was about five miles offshore. I remember now that the man who owned the boat would always manage two things. He would manage to be drunk, without any of us seeing him take a drink, and swear to us that he hadn't, and he would almost always manage to foul up the engine, and spend an hour tinkering with it, as we drifted towards the open sea.

Still it was good fishing. We would use lures or bits of herring and perch for bait, and ride the swells most of the day, with the point of Portage Island visible.

I loved fishing mackerel in the big boats in those early days, in shorts and bare feet—feet that had become so toughened I could run along the rocky Shore Road for a mile to get a loaf of bread. At night in our little cottage, when I was eight or nine, I would lie in bed and listen to the wind whistling off the dark and fearsome bay. I was going to become a fisherman and know the sea. And then perhaps my ancestry, or some other mysterious inclination, would draw me to the fir- and spruce-armoured woods, the sound of the river rushing around suicidal bends and cedar swamps. This, of course, was not so much a love of nature, I was to discover, but a response to the love of mankind. It might be sought in solitary ways, but in all ways that counted searching far-off places to fish seemed always to carry with it a love of humanity.

The sea and the river are both laden with traditions—absolutely proud, fearless, and different. I have come to know men who had grown up on our river and could canoe, blindfolded through rapids, but never saw our bay; and I have met men who spent their lives fishing lobster in ten-foot swells, but became claustrophobic when they could see the other side of a stream because everything was closing in on them.

This happened to a man I know who came down to my cottage, at the mouth of the bay, to collect the driftwood that had washed up on our beach. He was an older man, about 70, from Bellefond who worked most of the day with a chainsaw, cutting the huge logs and carrying them over to the one-ton truck. He looked out at the great water, shimmering in the

July sunshine and leaving in its mist mirages of old ships and islands that weren't really there.

"So this is the bay," he said. "By God, this is where the river runs to, and the salmon come from. I never knew it was like this." What surprised me is what always surprises me about these meetings. In a real way, in an ultimate way, I who had by that time travelled the world had seen not much more, or had not too many more experiences, that could count for anything than he himself had, who had lived almost all his days in a four- or five-mile track of woods, with a trap line and a bucksaw.

Three

THERE ARE THOSE WHO live near the woods, within a hat's throw of a stream or a fine salmon pool, and never discover them. My father's father died when my father was four years old. And in the truest sense my father was an orphan. He never knew about the woods. He didn't own a camp. He had no knowledge of the great empire of the northern woods that spread in all compass readings on all sides of him.

In the late spring, I watched as other kids got ready to go fishing or came home from fishing trips. In the night air they would bring the trout out of their fishing baskets and lay them on the cool grass. Sometimes hearing them come home I would run out in my pyjamas to see these trout laid out, signifying the mystical and haunted streams far off in the distance.

I was a town boy. And my father owned a business downtown and went to work in a suit and tie.

His world consisted of approximately eight blocks. As far as serious fishing was concerned, I may as well have been living in downtown Toronto.

The boys who fished with their dads would look on me as someone who knew nothing, a neophyte. This angered me. It angered me because they were right.

There was an *idea* of salmon fishing, of fly-fishing, that their judgemental scorn allowed me to see at a very early age. I was practised enough in detection of ridicule, but there was also the scent in the air of patronizing knowledge and just a little money. Not that these boys had any more money than I. But they had come in contact at a certain level with the idea of fish, and the fishing men, and understood *this*: the idea that fly-fishing was linked at some certain level, from some place, England or Scotland, to quite a privileged world. Not just a physical world; a monied world where in the search for game fish money was never spoken about, or perhaps only whispered about, at the end of the day. It took money to be rugged and get fish. Perhaps not for the people I grew up beside, but for certain people that they knew. Certain people who may have riparian rights to certain waters and pools. That did not *diminish* these people at all, but it only said what is always said: there is an affordability by a certain class (in a country where class is supposedly obsolete) where fishing takes on the splendour of gaming—not unlike the fox hunt. And that these laws and associations and riparian rights are jealously guarded. In the long run this may protect the fish that spawn in those privileged waters. But then again it may not. It may cause more resentment and resistence if it is perceived to be an elitist sport by those who feel they are not a part of it.

This duality has always fascinated me. That is, this understanding of camps with waitresses and cooks in white uniforms (my maternal grandmother was one) and guides in ties (my uncle was one).

But it is quite complicated. It does not diminish these men who come in search of these fish, but it shows a tiered society in which activity functions—the cultivated man as fisherman.

Each man (more so a generation ago than now) who goes to a camp of this kind finds that he is expected to play the role, whether he wants to or not, of a gentleman. Even if it is as simple a gesture as being helped in or out of a canoe, the role is somehow preordained. The guides expect the sport to play out his role, and he is driven not so much by privilege as by tradition to accept it. This is a generalization, of course, but all generalizations have a certain premise. This premise is as much a part of fly-fishing in camps like those particular ones on the Restigouche as anything else about fly-fishing. It is at times, and can be seen as, a wonderful parlour drama.

But this was really a later observation. In a more complicated way, those nights of running into the yard in my pyjamas to see the bountiful luck of other boys told me that friends of mine knew of another world—a privileged but *natural* world of the river that my father had been denied in his youth because of the death of his father; a knowledge that he was unable to share with me, even though he tried clumsily to do so.

He would take us fishing one Sunday a year in a dull green flat-bottom boat. And even now, in his old age, he remembers this with fondness. But he had no great notions or inclinations towards that world of fly-fishing. Still he offered us the best he could of the world he knew. Even a few years ago he admitted he did not know what a fly rod was. And how can he be blamed, never having seen or used one.

So, Mr. Simms, the next-door neighbour, older than my father, as old as my mother's older brothers, became my first link, my first real link with fly-fishing. The world of fly-fishing, the smell of the rods, the colour of flies, the tin boxes.

Mr. Simms worked in the woods in the winter, and lived in camps. In the summer he went off by himself with a tent. His hands were battered and his fingers twisted. He had one pipe and one tobacco pouch. He had one tin cup for drinking tea, commemorating the coronation of Elizabeth II. He carried it with him always.

He would go far up on the Sevogle and live alone, a life of a hermit, with a Coleman stove and tin cup, fly boxes and salmon rods. He would go into the woods for days and forge rapids, walk or canoe rivers, often without meeting a soul. The great dramas of his life would be played out alone. And then he would return with fish to boil, or smoke with hickory wood. He would study the river for one purpose—to find the salmon. He told me about the great pools—the square forks, the Big Hole at the mouth of the Sevogle, and pools far up on the Norwest that I was to see twenty years later—Moose Brook, American Pool.

All those places I was still to discover, from Caul's Pool to the Turnip Patch, from Big Birch to Clearwater, from the cave in to Clelland's, from Quarryville to the mouth of Dungarvon, Mr. Simms had already fished thirty or forty years before. I believe he was the first to show me an artificial fly, a Royal Coachman.

At the time I wondered how salmon could be fooled by it. It seemed to have in the very design of its feathers and body the imprint of man. This was my first impression of a salmon fly.

The process of fly-fishing suddenly seemed to require a great amount of rhythm and patience and dedication for which the common man didn't have time. Not the common man like Mr. Simms. So it seemed to me like a deception—and the deception was that Mr. Simms was fooling himself into thinking he was doing something natural when he was really doing something ornate and craftlike. So it must be craftsmen—not woodsmen—who really liked and were attracted to fly-fishing. Earls and princes perhaps, but not men like Mr. Simms who ran out log drives in the spring.

Except it *was* Mr. Simms who showed me his Royal Coachman.

These feelings hung with me for a while, and still return now and again when I meet certain individuals who fish as if they were part of an academy.

I didn't tell Mr. Simms these complicated feelings at that time because they were not entirely clear to me, and because he loved the great assortment of flies he was showing me. But the flies in his fly box, with their wonderful deceptive dressings, did not seem to complement the great natural woods, the vast rivers that these men explored for fish. Salmon fishing was supposedly linking men once again with their natural self. It took me a while to realize that tying flies in order to salmon fish was not only, in the end, *natural* but an *art.*

An art—far more than digging worms out in the garden. It is through this process of fly-tying that a person got to know the fish and themselves far better, and became more personally attached to the river. Through the fly they either trusted or had tied themselves, they faced a challenge that becomes quite philosophical, even if they themselves weren't philosophical about it. The wonder of this is that no two flies tied true are ever the same. A Green Butt Butterfly on a number 8 hook tied by my friend at 7:45 on February 3, 1976 is never the same as the Green Butt Butterfly tied on a number 8 hook at 8:00 that same night.

The fly becomes in all its ornate beauty of regulated simplicity an extension of the imagination, and knowledge of the fisherman in winter, for those fish he is seeking, in those months holed up in his basement or squirrelled away in his shed. He can see the fish in pools, and can guess how the fly will move in a forty-five degree arc towards them, how he will rest a fish that has just boiled, how he will shorten up his line to fish down to it once again. This fly-tying process becomes, with snow over the window ledges and the river blocked and soundless for miles, an act of faith and will.

Mr. Simms had a good deal of will and knowledge and a thousand flies. He had been stranded for days in the snow one winter. He dug himself into the snow, and waited the blizzard out drinking pine-needle tea. He had worked his way through many fine difficulties, had been trapped by a forest fire when he was a young man and stayed the whole night in the water.

He missed a finger and had rough calloused hands. He wore, like old woodsmen of the generation gone, Humphrey pants and a checkered woodshirt, which always smelled of kerosene, spruce, and tobacco. He had known no other life. That people now flew off to Toronto or New York or Paris on a daily basis to do business would be as foreign to him as space travel. Nor do I think, except for the finger, he missed much. He was, and always will be, the embodiment of a Miramichier; proud, conscious of others, fearless within the bounds of a physical environment, filled with humour, and yet somewhat shy. When he worked in the camps years before, the average day would start off at five o'clock. In the camps and with the working conditions of a generation or two ago it is amazing more men didn't go mad. Certainly some did.

He liked to tell me about Saint John, N.B., and how high the tides were there—the highest tides in the world—and that some day he would get on a bus and go to see them. I did not want to tell him that I myself had been to Saint John with my family, had seen these tides, where boats rested on the bottom of the bay after the tide went out. Like most true rural men, he was proud of small gifts from God.

He called me, in his gruff old voice, "the little Christ child" because of the pitchfork going through my left foot a few years back. He had made the mistake—just as many others in my neighbourhood had—of believing that this is how I had become lame. He didn't know the real reason—my mother falling on her stomach when she was pregnant, and causing a brain haemorrhage—and I did not volunteer the information.

So I always tried to be as modest and as pleasant as I could when I sat there. But sometimes I would tell him my left foot ached, when it didn't, and I would look sorrowfully about, and then I would look up at the birds flying, as if I could never be as free, yet my spirit soared (or something like that). So it must have been a very poignant moment.

"Christ child, you've got to go fishing," he would say, his lips trembling when he looked at me, and then bending over to spit out his plug.

"I know," I would say. "I will—but now I'm a little tired."

The truth is this: All my life men and women (except those individuals who actually hate me) have found in me some endearing quality that they wish to protect, and Mr. Simms was one of these people. He told me about his son, who went away and never came back, and he would get me ice cream and sit and look at me, and ask if my foot was still hurting.

"Not so much now," I would say. "Thank you, sir."

"God almighty, Christ child—don't call me sir. I'm just ol' Alvin Simms."

Then I would have to go to confession. I would tell the priest that I had lied about my foot aching.

"Why would you ever do that?"

"They all think I'm the little Christ child."

There would be a disturbed silence on the priest's side of the box.

"Did you ever get fishing yet?" Mr. Simms would ask.

I would have to tell him that no I hadn't, but that I would go in a few days time. That was always the story.

One day when his twin brother came to visit, Mr. Simms said, "Why don't you take the little Christ child fishing?"

I looked up with a feeling of dread and expectation. I immediately thought that though I had bragged about wanting to learn to fly-fish I wouldn't be able to do it. It would be the same as skating for hockey, or baseball, or volleyball, or anything else I had ever tried. I would try to do it and find out with my limitations that I could not do it. This was the curse of my childhood and took me a long while to overcome.

I would be up in a tent somewhere in the middle of nowhere and I would be left behind, frightened of being eaten almost immediately by a bear.

But his brother looked around, as if trying to see where the little Christ child was, and then saw this miserable skinny specimen sitting in front of him.

"No, I can't do that," he said laconically. "I'm going in for the week. Why don't he go become fishers of men?"

This rather blasphemous statement aside, I liked Mr. Simms's brother. They worked in the woods all their lives and had shared the same woman. This started at a dance when they were sixteen and they continued to try to fool her their whole lives. They both took her out, and they both decided that they were married to her.

"She married you but she thought you was me!"

"LIAR!"

They made a mad dash for home when they left the woods, trying to get out before the other, jostling and bumping one another, and trying to force each other off the road.

She wrote Ann Landers about this for advice, because she couldn't decide. To her, they both seemed exactly the same.

I remember Mr. Simms's diary only vaguely—as you remember things from the past by a peculiar kind of association that is never straightforward. Mr. Simms's diary will always remind me, in a circuitous way, of nuns. And of school. Of Sister Saint John Daniel and Mother Saint David because of how his diary was written in pencil. And the nuns had taught both of us to write.

In this diary there were small sketches of a man—perhaps of Simms himself—standing along a bank of a river, with the line of his fishing rod taut. The water and the rocks were just a few discernible pencil strokes, but these pencil strokes showed man against nature, far up on some river bend alone, as well as any I've seen sketched.

One day, many years later, when I told him I had poled the North Pole Branch from Lizard Brook down eight miles with my friend Peter, in search of trout (I was quite proud of this because it was such a hard go that day with the water low), he replied that I should have poled *up* from Lizard Brook nine miles to find the trout I was then seeking. That is, pole up *against* the current, because he had done that for years as a young man. The pride my friend and I had in navigating down seemed less splendid after that.

Mr. Simms's diary was written in pencil, and was faded. As long as I knew him he never used a pen. It was as if a pen was too grandiose. There was always an old yellow bitten pencil in his kitchen drawer, where the diary lay. The house is now gone. It has been gone perhaps for twenty years.

The diary too might have disappeared by now. But the memories are still in that part of experience, as saddened by time as old black-and-white pictures of trout or salmon at a camp. And in the grain of those old pictures there always seems to me to be undisclosed knowledge about the men who fished those fish. Whether they took too many, were unthinking, were just, were patient, were professional. All this seems to be in the pictures though the pictures might show man and fish that have been both dead for forty years. Nothing one does, in this way or in any way, will go undiscovered. That is the secret truth about fishing or hunting.

For a time I became Simms's eyes and ears about who was getting fish, and he would tell me stories. He told me a story about his cousins who once stole a camp from him, and how he got back at them. It was a very interesting story and I was to relate it years later to my friend on the South Branch Sevogle one night in late July. I do not know if my friend believed this story nor am I certain that I do. Mr. Simms was a man replete with stories, about fishing and hunting and horses, and log drives, and winters, and ghosts in the woods.

I would go back and relate these stories to kids as if it were me who had invented them. I had to do this, at that time, for I had nothing else to tell.

But I did not get fishing salmon then or for a long while after.

I would go over to the house and ask my father to take me fishing. He would be having his noon-hour nap, with a blanket pulled over his head, his left hand hanging down over the side of the bed. I would pick up his hand, feel the pulse, and drop it back where it was. Then I would go try to find something else to do.

That year, in late October, just after my birthday, I had gone for a Saturday hunt with my father—while Gordon and his friend had gone with their fathers to their hunting camp on the Little Souwest. Gordon was a snob of all the right proportions and calibre. An egotist of manner even at twelve. A person who knew the right and the wrong way to do things. Even the way to talk about what one talked about *in* the woods, or about the river.

A person then who knew the price of everything, and the

value of nothing. A rather hard indictment to hold against a boy of twelve, but there you are. I'm not sure I knew that I held it then. But I suppose I did that day we as childhood neighbours went hunting in separate vehicles to separate places.

We both arrived home at the same time—just about seven at night.

They had a twelve-point buck in the back of their truck. The buck probably weighed 220 pounds. I went over and looked at it. It had been shot in the foreshoulder at dusk, as it made its way back to a rut above a little stream. Though the stream was opened there was an inch or so of snow down. The area in back of it was in gloom, with small spruce and maple cuts. It was October 24, 1961; that was the day that the buck was shot. There is always in my memory a smell of gunpowder in the fall that traces the wind and sky.

Gordon had seen it shot by his father who now sported a three-day growth of beard.

I saw through the dark the yellow leaves (there was as yet no snow in town, even though in the woods snow had fallen), the lights from their garage, the very palpable hint of excitement in the air that, along with the gunpowder, was always persistent in my memory of autumn.

They lifted the buck from the truck, cut holes in its back

leg tendons, and hung it from the rafters of the garage, and there they began the process of taking the hide off it.

Gordon walked about touching the hide that was being pulled back from the buck's layer of fat. He had an important and elemental role to fill at that moment, the son of a successful hunter. And as all children, when I looked at this deer, I never thought of the animal being dead; I always thought of it being alive—how splendid it must have been.

It was the third deer Gordon's father had shot in two years.

I could not stand this. I was filled with jealousy. So when Gordon and I went out into the night air I said—not loud enough to be heard by the men, but neither in a whisper—"We got a deer too."

"You did," Gordon said, and he actually believed me. Which made me feel terrible.

Then I said, "Ya, well, we'll see you later."

"Let me come over and see it," Gordon said, and he was excited and happy for me.

"Oh no—look—it's not like your deer. It's more littler—and stuff like that there."

"What do you mean, 'stuff like that there'?" Gordon said suspiciously. And over he followed me to my house. There was no way I could shake him. And so I went around to the back, looking down into the cellar window. I pointed to something in the corner—it was a carpet my mother had just beaten to death with a broom.

"That's the hide right there," I said. "We'll make a lot of deerflies with that ol' hide."

He looked at me, Gordon did, with such a quizzical look of profound embarrassment at my own lying idiocy that I have never quite gotten over it.

Of course Gordon was my nemesis. He was always better than I was at anything he did—that was a given. But his father was also better at what he did than my father.

So I had to make up stories about things my father did. I told them my father was a war ace, and shot down eight planes—I wanted to say eighteen planes, but I settled for eight.

They were imperturbable people, hard to impress.

His father was a mechanical engineer with the mines, so I suppose he could do things that my father couldn't even dream of doing—because of narcolepsy, he slept fifteen hours a day.

The one thing I was able to do, however, when I went with my father hunting or fishing, was something most kids would give a fish for.

"Do you mind driving?" Dad would ask.

"Not at all—not even a little bit," I would say.

"Don't tell your mom," he would say.

"Mum's the word," I would answer.

Putting two pillows under my behind, so I was able to see over the steering wheel, I drove along while my father snoozed. Once I took a wrong road and ended up at a house. I was inside, eating a peanut butter sandwich and playing cards with an old lady, when my father woke in the yard. In he came, to see me dressed up for fishing and playing snap with an old lady called Massie, while the grandfather sat in the corner by the old wood stove, lifting the lid every now and then to spit his plug.

It was nice to drive a car and play snap with new friends, but I never got a fish.

Four

THE NEXT SUMMER I walked downtown—on at least eight separate occasions—to the hunting and fishing tackle shop. I would stand inside the door, looking at the knives and flies, looking at the three canoes for sale—an eighteen-foot, a fifteen-foot, and a fourteen-foot imitation birch bark (the one that caught my eye). Many other kids would do this too, and one, Peter McGrath, who became one of my friends, would march out on his own as soon as he could and discover this fishing and hunting world by himself.

I, on the other hand, would think of myself in those

canoes, fishing those pools, casting those rods, without having any idea of how I was going to transport myself from one place to the other, or how to fish once I got there.

The days were hot, the sidewalks still. The clothing stores and general store doors were open and men stood in small groups lazing away the day.

On Saturdays I went to work at a grocery store cleaning out the garbage bin—standing waist high in boxes and cans and dirt—for $1.80. And I would put that money away for the canoe I never got.

I would take my spin cast and practise on the lawn, until one day a boy showed me his fly rod, and told me that all fishermen used fly rods, and that only kids—like *me*—used spin casts. I already knew this because of what Mr. Simms told me.

So I decided then and there to get a fly rod, or to give up fishing.

At eighteen, I bought a second-hand fly rod, perhaps the heaviest I ever owned, with large wire eyes. I don't remember what kind of rod it was, just that one afternoon it was in my possession, with an old yellow line on an old black reel. So one September morning, my first year of university, I trudged out to the Nashwaak River. I hitchhiked out to a pool, walked many miles, and to my amazement raised a salmon.

I had just thrown my fly at the water and *splash,* this huge fish came up and rolled over it. I never *rested* the fish, of course, because I didn't know anything about it. I threw the fly right back and something took. Unfortunately it was a parr, and the barb of my fly went through its eye. In fact, I may have been slightly fearful of hooking a salmon. When I look back at it now, I wouldn't for the life of me have known exactly what to do. I was also so far out into the rapid that day, that I definitely had a struggle getting back, walking up along the bar. If I had hooked that fish, I might have been in a real predicament. But there is a certain amount of instinct too that comes with fishing, and many have caught their first fish in similar conditions.

Yet I was to fish for the rest of that day. I was to dream about that salmon at night. I was to skip classes and walk twelve miles back to the Nashwaak, to try my luck again, without success. But I believed I was a fisherman.

I don't know what kind of fly I was using. I think it was a Black Ghost. The Nashwaak is a level meandering river, with some well-known beautiful pools. It is a late river, so September fishing is productive, and skipping class seemed to me as natural an occurrence in my life as most things.

Then winter came and I lay my fly-fishing rod and my excursions away. A few times that winter I got back home, and would look at the frozen river, capped with snow, and think of the dark water of spring. I as yet didn't tell anyone I had fished for salmon, but I listened to various young men talking about it. How they knew a fish would take, how they knew exactly where that fish was, how they had poled downriver after a rain when the water was dropping, etc., etc. It all seemed as exotic as big-game hunting.

Early the next summer on the Miramichi I took my salmon rod, and got a few flies, and went to Quarryville, waded out into the water in my jeans, and made a cast, and lo and behold I hooked a big fish. I thought it was a big fish. It turned out to be nothing more than a common sucker, but it weighed about a pound.

I then waded out a little more, threw another cast, and my entire line fell off the reel. There it went, floating out from me twenty feet away. I looked first to my right and then to my left to see if anyone had actually seen my rod fall apart and went home for repairs.

That same summer I went down to the Church River, near my old cottage at Burnt Church. I walked up along the bank, getting my line tangled in the trees, and then waded towards a pool. The pool came full into a dogleg turn, and passed a large birch windfall. The day was sunny, with the scent of spruce and clover, the bank of the river was reddish, and small turbulent eddies swept along in a golden hue.

Everywhere on Church River there was the life of the north woods, which so many of us take so much for granted. As I came into the doglegged pool, I looked down.

About my feet were dozens of large sea trout coming up to spawn. Unfortunately I had no idea what fly to use, and I put on such a large streamer the trout had no interest. When I cast it over them they simply moved out of its way, as unconcerned with it as they were with me. Perhaps I should have thought just for a second or two, looked over to the flow of water, and studied the hatches, the small, winged insects. That is what everyone always says they did, when they were a neophyte like myself.

But I did not do that. I kept turning about in circles studying the fish, until I got dizzy, literally.

Finally unable to entice them, I sat down and watched them move through and into the pool. And then after a while they were gone. They had moved out of that pool and went on upriver.

I sat near the bank drinking a beer, disgusted with how nonchalantly they ignored me, and how incapable I was of doing anything. About an hour later an older man came wading down the river, with a fedora hat littered with bright tiny flies, wearing hip waders and carrying a trout basket.

"Any luck?" he said.

"None at all," I admitted.

He came over and sat beside me, offered me a Player's cigarette, opened his knapsack, and showed me four or five trout he had taken, each about three pounds, their bodies whiter and limper in death. He was using tiny nymph flies, so tiny he used thick glasses to thread them through his leader, and fishing under the limbs of trees sweeping down over small runs. To his advantage, he had a tiny trout rod, about six and a half feet long.

"Well, they're in the river now," he said. "Strange you didn't find them—but you'll find yours some day."

He stayed a moment and then moved downstream and around the bend out of sight.

After he left I was to fish until almost dark, my fly clumsily splashing the water and scaring everything that remained in the pool.

I married a woman from Bartibog, that gem of a river, when we were both still kids. It is strange to think that I passed her house and her as a child a thousand times on my way to and from Church River when I was a child and never knew her then. Or that our paths must have crossed even before and after that. That we were at the same church picnics in the summer—perhaps no more than a dozen feet from one another.

It even seems to me that I stood beside her in church one day when we were only ten, neither of us knowing the other.

Peggy was the person who finally prodded me into asking for some kind of direction in my fishing life. Her uncles and her cousins were all good or fairly good fishermen, but her own family didn't fly-fish. She told me one day to ask one of her cousins and added that I was at the point where I was going to have to ask someone or give up.

"You should ask Peter or David," she said.

Peter McGrath was a friend of my younger brother, and David Savage was Peggy's first cousin. Both of them fished, and they had often talked about fishing, getting fish, and knowing where the fish were, and I was always too shy, and also too stubborn, to ask them anything about it.

I met Peter McGrath the next night and had a beer with him.

"I'm sick and tired of worms," I finally blurted.

"Who's a worm?" he said looking at me.

"Oh, no one's a worm. I just want to use a fly."

"Oh, yer talking about fishing," Peter said, "Well, I'll show you where to go—"

"You will?"

"I said I would," he said, as he always did, answering people's questions directly. Everything Peter says has a relevance to the moment more than to the past or future. He is in that part, like most men who are active and prefer action, to a degree that many are not, responsible for himself and what he says.

And like all the men I have met and admired on the Miramichi, for their dexterity in the woods, Peter does not *read* the woods as a biologist or a naturalist or a conservationist might. Not that there is anything wrong with how they might read it, or relate it to us. Biologists and naturalists have worlds of information to provide us, about the greater problems the fish stocks face, but I have not yet met one who actually feels the woods about him, like some of the fishermen and hunters I know.

Peter, like others, is comfortable in the woods, to the degree that his being *becomes* a part of it. That is the truest testing for natural ability, in both fishing and hunting. Or any occupation.

However, I would get to know a few pools, and then when Peter got tired of showing me I could hike out on my own, maybe even get my own truck. Of course, as always in a person's imagination, I imagined fish, and my own canoe and truck and everything else.

Fishing is a poetic act. There are a great many books that talk about the poetry of fishing, and yet silence might be the best way to understand it. Only to know that it is there, within each person, in an infinite number of ways. What draws men and women to fly-fishing is its testing of self-reliance, co-ordination, strength, and skill, combined at a variety of levels with the notion of a poetic grasp of the world. No one I have met describes taking a fish or fishing for salmon without in some way being poetic. They might not even know they are being poetic when they talk of the eddies, the falls, the way the water has flooded an area, the banks of the river, how a fish moves from its lay and rises for a fly.

When I started that year I had no car, let alone a truck. I had to tie blood knots with one hand and my teeth. I had not been in a canoe since my uncle snapped that picture. I did not know anything of the Norwest, let alone the Little Souwest, the Sevogle or its branches. I told myself it did not matter.

Yet it mattered very much.

Since I was a boy I had always watched for the signs from other people when they spoke about sport. Skating is easy, they would say. Skiing is easy. Swimming is easy. Rock climbing is easy. Baseball is easy.

"Fishing is easy," Peter told me. But I *know* all the levels of difficulty attached to easy, when you can barely open your left hand. Then again, left hand be damned.

The first day I went salmon fishing, since those few occasions on the Nashwaak—in an old pair of waders with an old rod, with a small plastic dish filled with four flies: two butterflies, a Black Ghost, and a Green Butt Bear Hair—I caught a grilse about three and a half pounds.

It was a warm day in June as we drove to the Stickney Road where we could walk into the Norwest Miramichi. Peter had a Russian-made Lada truck, which you could take a sledge-hammer to without denting, but which was also incomprehensibly pernickety. We parked at the gate and began a three-mile walk into Dr. Wilson's pool. I had not seen Wilson's Pool before then. On either side of the road the trees, stunted spruce and maple, waved slightly in the early-morning heat and beaver dams had flooded the road at various places. There were the on-again, off-again faraway calls of ravens. The day was sunny, the sky with distant nebulous clouds that seemed to dissipate before our eyes, and stretches of the road were miraged with pools of water that would fade away to nothing as we walked through them going to where the real water must be. Now and then a colourful bird would glide into a landing a few yards ahead, as silent as the mirages we walked through.

Wearing the waders made it twice as hot, and tore at our feet. But finally we turned from Stickney Road which would lead one down to Stickney Pool, and we went, along a cooler more overgrown road, towards Wilson's Pool where an old camp stood. The camp was still in fairly good shape, and sat on a flat about twelve yards from the water. Poplars and maples grew about it, and it was dogged at the back by bog and spruce. But it had never been swept away. I stared at the river. How surely, and unconscious of us, and the trees above it, it flowed. As unconscious of self as all great things are, as some of the best fishermen and women are.

The river was quite full and flowed quickly, and was not as wide as I thought it would be. But then I remembered a past time long ago when, as a boy of twelve, Mr. Simms told me about this place, and how he took a salmon here, and I realized that he had described it exceptionally well to me. It was as if the salmon somehow still existed, and always would. That the river, this great Norwest Miramichi, proved to us that life was infinite and continuous.

I looked at the camp and thought the same thing. The patched walls inside, the faint smell of bark and charcoal, the scent of sun hitting the roof reminded me of the story Mr. Simms had told about his sawed-off cousins, and how they had stolen his camp, and how he got it back. I decided I would tell that story to Peter some day. The camp stood in silence at the edge of this world. The world about us was in bloom, with wild daisies and foot-high ferns, the buds sprouted out into early leaf.

"We'll get fish here," Peter told me, as I was thinking this and he was reading the water, "I guarantee it."

Well, guarantee is good, I thought, but since I had only cast a fly rod once or twice before, I was a little uncertain about it.

I heard the rapids at the top of this fine pool as we walked up to it. And there is nothing more thrilling to a fisherman than that sound.

The river was still high, over the grassy path, the water swift and beer brown flowing over the boulders that dotted the river, leaving most of them submerged, their tips like icebergs.

As we approached the pool we could see some commotion. It was strange that the first person I would ever meet on the river was my wife's first cousin, David Savage, and his dog, Blue. The little mutt was running back and forth on the shore, where Savage had his Norwest canoe pulled up, and at the lower part of the pool he was playing a fish. His rod was bent over, his line was tight in the water, as if it was hooked to a boulder. But now and again that line would move, as the fish moved, and the reel would sing. The fish had jumped a few times, but was now staying down, moving with the current and then turning into it. Then it would take long runs and Savage's line would go out.

I sat down on the bank and watched him, and had as much fun doing that as fishing. After another ten minutes, David landed the fish, a female salmon about eight pounds. He had taken it on a Rusty Rat, a small dusty rust-coloured fly.

It seemed incomprehensible to a novice like myself that a fly that small could take a fish that large. Or that the invisible leader wouldn't snap away. And I might have said this when he later showed the fly and leader to me. But it was a number 6 Rusty Rat and, consequently, was a big fly compared to some used later on in the summer. Also a ten-pound test would go down to a six-pound test as the water conditions got lower after June, and the summer went on.

Another thing I was bemused by was how this water could hide fish that size, even if it was heavy darkish water that day.

I suppose I could take a moment to think of Karen Blixen's description of fish in her story collection *Antedote of Destiny*, and how they are perfect representatives of the best of God's world. How they live in a kind of three-dimensional world of space and time, that there is no up or down for them, or sideways. They move as surely as any of God's great creatures, and the salmon is one of the surest of all God's fish. On the Miramichi, fish *means* salmon. So if you ask someone if they have seen any *fish* and they say, "No, but I got a few trout," it is not at all a contradiction.

People I met that day, and in the months to come, I would meet for years, and get to know some of them well. But some of them I would know only as others who haunted our rivers of grace. In the years to come, around a turn on a faraway branch, I would meet someone who I had not seen since the frost came the year before. There he or she was again, working their way through a pool, throwing a wonderful line unconscious of themselves. Or perhaps they would be offshore, in among the ferns, because they had spotted in the dew a patch of wild berries. You would become close to them by this aspect of humanity even though you may or may not have spoken to them very much.

Way up on the Norwest, where I fished for the first few years, I would often meet a man from Chatham, who came the same time as we did every year. Then as the year went along, we switched rivers—he going to a river some place else, and I wouldn't see him again, until he reappeared early the next season, as if he had come out of the earth. I would look up and he'd be there, wearing the same waders and hat, giving us the same rough smile.

We would talk and have coffee, take turns moving through the pool. Once we boiled a fish on the side of the shore in an old bent aluminum pot on his Coleman stove, in the pouring rain. His wife had made him brown bread and molasses cookies, which we ate along with the freshly boiled grilse. He lazed on the beach staring at the hypnotic water and talked about bringing his son with him. That he was going to teach his son how to fish as soon as he got a little older.

Then one year at that same time he did not come back. And we found out he had died of a heart attack sometime that winter at the age of thirty-eight. The shadows moved on the trees as we worked our way through the pool ourselves. I stared over my shoulder to the little rocky beach where we had boiled our grilse with such ceremonial laughter—I thought of his son.

Five

THE MIRAMICHI IS A multiple of rivers and streams intertwined. There is no one place to go, there are literally hundreds of places. Although one place might remind you of another, all places are essentially different, have their own spirit attached to them. The Little Souwest is much different than the Norwest, and different kinds of fishermen travel these branches. But some people travel all rivers.

Peter McGrath often viewed this world of his, the Miramichi, as a continual kaleidoscope of possibilities.

Hunting or fishing, Peter is like this. For instance,

hunting: I'd be sitting near a rut mark, and Peter would walk up.

"Let's go," he'd say. "I'm compressed." (*Compressed* rather than *depressed* because he believes it is a better adjective. And I have come to agree with him.)

"Why—why are you compressed? What is there to be compressed about? There is nothing in the world to be compressed about. There's a buck right here. Where the hell are you thinking of now?"

Peter would point with his finger to some unknown space far away, around bends and denizens of the late-autumn forest, the sky like grey slate, and all about us the hushed whispers of tiny flakes of snow.

"Are you slightly hyperactive, Peter?" I asked him one day, up on the south branch of the Sevogle, after we'd just walked five miles upriver from where we had parked the truck.

"No, the fish are," he said, pointing finally to four or five grilse in the bottom part of the pool we were just coming to. As I said, he answers always directly and with purpose.

So that first day, without throwing a line at Wilson's Pool, we turned and walked three miles back to the Lada truck, because Peter didn't feel we'd have luck where we were. And who was I to disagree, not knowing one pool from the other.

I had worn my waders for two hours and had yet to stand in the water. Suddenly it seemed as if I were not so much on a fishing expedition, but in the French Foreign Legion: March or die.

As a matter of fact, there was a large puddle on the Stickney Road I felt like sucking dry.

We headed upriver to the open pool on the stony brook stretch that early summer day, years ago, generations of fish ago, past the millions of leaves, on those hundreds of thousands of trees.

I was in no hurry to get out of the truck again. But at any rate I didn't have to be in much of a hurry, for Peter was prepared to drive another thirty-five miles (or so it seemed to me) through the woods to get us to where he wanted us to go.

"We'll get fish today—I guarantee it," he said to keep my interest alive. The road got narrower and narrower; the trees closer; the rocks bigger.

When we finally came near the river Peter was again worried. And this was my first introduction to the guessing game he played with himself always.

That is, were those *fresh* tire tracks ahead of us, which meant that someone else, out of the dozen or so people who fished this area, was in before us.

But when we came to the end of the old road, there was

no other car in sight. We parked at the end of the road, got out of the truck in the June silence and got ready. I put the line through my rod and put on a Red Butt Butterfly, and headed down the long path over the steep bank with him, and then up along the shore about a quarter mile to B&L Pool, or Brandy Landing Pool.

The path we walked was wide enough to make us feel that we were at home somewhere. The sun came down on it through the trees, everything smelled of pine nettles, the ground itself was bathed in copper, and when we got about halfway down this path, I could see the rapids of the small falls on my lower left, and heard it as a constant rush. The water was still high, it being late spring, and over the bank. There was something (and this always struck me) completely self-absorbed about the woods, the trees and the water which allowed people to travel over or upon them, to walk through it or near it, but to rarely be a part of it.

"What river is this?" I asked.

"This is the same river—just a few miles up," Peter said.

We walked up to the pool in silence.

Brandy Landing is a pool with a rocky bank on the far side, and set off at the top and bottom by rocks. The flow of water at the top is rough, it enters over a cascade of rock, and at the bottom it flows swiftly enough to entice fish on their long journey from the ocean, to rest in the cool shade, when they come into it. A fly works well except at the top middle, where it has a tendency to bow your line, unless you fish it from the middle of the top rapid. From the top quarter of the pool down to the large rock on the far side fish lie. There are three or four major hot spots, though on a good day fish can be anywhere. It is part of the stony brook stretch of the Norwest Miramichi, and as such has been closed for a few years, now part of the Crown reserve. But anyone who is lucky enough to get to fish it is in for wonderful moments.

I let Peter go in ahead of me, and followed behind. He pointed to where I should start.

I cast my first cast (the line—all ten feet or so—went over my head and back to the water) and hooked a grilse.

"I think I got one on," I said.

"What do you mean, you think you got one on," Peter said suspiciously.

"I think I got something on," I said, as the line bowed, and the fish tried to move out of the pool and upriver—which meant he was probably leaving the pool when it saw my fly skimming across the surface of the top rapid and took.

"My God, you got a fish on," Peter said in amazement. "How did you do that?"

"I was born for this," I said. "I was absolutely born for this. Now what do I do?"

"I was absolutely born for this" would come back to haunt the hell out of me over the next few years. It would haunt my aching feet and tired arms and the knots in my leader.

Peter came back and watched me play it. The fish, though only a grilse (a young salmon) and not a large one, was still incredibly strong. It was as strong as any mackerel I played. In fact, it was strong enough that when it took I thought for a moment that I had snagged a rock (except instinctively one knows they have something alive at the end of the line).

"Keep your rod up or you'll lose it." And when the fish took to the air he yelled.

"Lower your rod or you'll snap your leader."

This went on for about ten minutes, and the fish slowly tired. I managed to do enough to keep it on, but I'm not exactly sure what it was I did. Finally it turned and rolled on its belly.

I managed to drag the fish up over the small lip of the bank. And I thought I was a fisherman. (Well, I didn't know I had just begun my quest.)

Later that week I went down to get some flies from David Savage. Though not a huge man he is very strong, with fingers that look too thick to tie the minute and wonderful flies he ties. Like most men, he poles the river, standing in the back of his Norwest canoe built for him by Ralph Mullin. It takes little for him to manoeuvre this canoe over rapids or between boulders. The great thing about poling is that you have more control than a paddle, and can stop the canoe dead, and change its direction in a hair. You can also see the river with the advantage of height, and notice a fish in the pool quicker.

The Norwest canoe is a heavy canoe but takes little to manoeuvre on this kind of river, our Norwest River which is a relatively small and swift river, and reminds me of the Padapedia, the river that runs along the border between Quebec and New Brunswick—or, I should say, the Padapedia reminds me of the Norwest Miramichi. (Save for the fact that the Norwest Miramichi has three times the fly-fishing pressure and is four times as productive.)

You have larger canoes to navigate the main Souwest Miramichi and the rivers like the Restigouche; both of these rivers have long large pools, and you also need to cast a longer line to cover your water. But the Norwest canoe handles extremely well and would do well on any river.

At that time David lived in a mobile home in Lower Newcastle, and had his fly-tying shop across the road. It was here he kept his fly-tying equipment and deer trophies, all kinds of purple and yellow and green feathers surrounded him, along with the fur from groundhogs, deer, and bear. He tied for a dozen different stores. He would tie two hundred dozen flies a year. He can tell a pattern by quickly looking at a new fly out of the corner of his eye, when he is up on the river, and remember it.

That night, long ago now, he was tying up a mouse to fish some trout. He had cleaned a trout the year before and had found three tiny mice in its belly.

Most summer evenings after supper, David would take his car and travel up the Bartibog just at twilight, when other people were going home. This is always the best time for trout fishing. He would go down a path to the pools hidden by bends and cedar trees, and orange in the twilight, begin to fish for trout in the swift currents under the alders and sweeping about small jams and windfalls where you need dexterity and precision to cast. His favourite area is far up the Bartibog River, at places where it isn't much wider than a stream, and has the colour of a cloudy beer. Great trout migrate there and are hidden in the evening shadows.

After supper the world takes on a different hue. It is suspended between light and darkness, and the evening becomes more and more still. Only the sound of the water over rocks, or trickling through the sweep of fallen branches, while the sunlight cools, the shadows moment by moment lengthen.

Then, just at dark, with the water entertaining a dozen variety of small hatches, David, using small nymph flies, number 12 or 14, would feel the pull on his line. He has a variety of flies he uses for trout, and I have used many of them in the last few years, on the Bartibog, Church, and Bay du Vin. Fishing trout this way is wonderful—perhaps, in memory, the finest fishing there is.

He would make his way out in the dark, back to his car, with four or five large trout, having fished the same spots others had fished two hours earlier with no luck.

I went back fishing with a few more flies. I felt I should have my own box of flies—to look professional.

Of course the only thing I couldn't quite do at that moment was cast a fly-rod line. It seemed to be a difficult proposition for me. And it hampered my plans. I focused all my energy upon learning something that to others came so easily (or so I thought).

I could cast three or four yards all right, but anything beyond that I was in trouble. I knew where the fish might lie. I was in a quandary over how to get my fly to reach them. I spent long hours—and hours and hours—still learning this. To make matters worse, everyone told me that a six-year-old could cast three hundred yards or more—that it wasn't strength, it was simply dexterity. But that was the problem. I have always had strength—dexterity was my problem. And I was in dread that I would meet a six-year-old, and his five-year-old sister on the river who would show me up.

So I practised every chance I got.

The rod is another extension of imagination. The fish that takes hangs off it by the slender line and, much more slender leader, and bows it down like a springboard and, like a springboard it has a ton of force. The fly is cast, the movement of the arm is generally from ten o'clock to one o'clock, and the line rolls out and lays down. That is how fishermen describe it. To lay down a cast. A line that is cast at a forty-five-degree angle into the pool is the most proper, though people have variances. Some will determine it is better to cast straight out at an eighty- or ninety-degree angle, but the fly will not work half so well. The fly will move from that forty-five-degree angle along an arc until it stands slack in front of you. By this time the fisherman has stripped his line, has moved his position by a foot or two, and is ready to pick up again. The fly raises in the air, the cast is lain down again and, in this way, the water is covered. No matter where you think the fish might or might not be, it is better to work your fly towards it. Even the minutest water missed can miss a fish. I discovered this one day fishing with a friend. On a certain stretch I thought I had covered the water fairly well. But my friend watched, borrowed my rod, went out and placed the fly exactly in an area no more than a few square inches I had missed. As soon as his fly touched I knew he would take a fish.

When the fish takes, you allow the rod to work. You hold your rod up until the fish jumps and then lower it, so as to take strain off the leader. You let the fish have its way until it is tired and slowly work it towards you, while backing into shore. Most people beach their fish on the Miramichi, and net them on the Restigouche. When a fish is beached the person will back up onto a shore, bringing the spent fish with him. But I've seen people—generally Nova Scotians—turn around and run to shore with the rod over their shoulder. The first time I saw someone do this, on the Renous, I thought they had gone mad with excitement.

But in learning how to use the rod I became aware of another side to fishing. There are those who have a degree of snobbishness about them and their fishing ability and judge you accordingly. This snobbishness can cross all class and cultural lines, but it is instantly aggravating when you run into it as a novice. If you meet it as a young fisherman, it can ruin a good day or a good season. The best thing is to try not to let it bother you. When I ran into it the first few years it was most often from people who themselves were worried about *belonging* in the world in some more exclusive way than you. An immaculate fisherman, a jurisprudent fisherman, a judgemental fisherman is somehow in some way an elitist and close-minded fisherman.

But my fishing life doesn't belong to them, and my stories, for the most part, are not about them.

WHEN HE WAS YOUNG, and had a young family to support, Peter McGrath, one July day, decided that the only way to know those branches of the great river was to walk them. To become, in a certain way, a part of them.

His determination was intensified by the fact that he did not have a canoe or a truck to travel in at that time. He had a car, and worked shift work, so he could only get to the river every so often.

When he was little he pleaded with his mother to take him hunting and fishing, because his father could not stand to hunt, to see anything hurt, and never fished. Peter once told me this story about himself as a little boy.

"One autumn afternoon we were up on the Renous highway," he told me. "My dad and mom and I were driving along. It was a Monday, and about four in the afternoon. We came around a turn, and a large buck was standing off on the side of the road. Dad had his rifle with him, and pulled the car over.

"There it is, Dad," he said. "Shoot it."

His father got out of the car, took the rifle from the back seat, put the shell in the chamber, and stood there. But he could really never bring himself to kill anything.

"Shoot it," Peter pleaded.

He lifted the rifle, aimed, and then looked back at his son.

"Shoot it," Peter said.

"I can't," his father said, almost apologetically.

"What do you mean you can't?" Peter whispered. "What do you mean, *can't.* There is no such thing as can't. Could shoot —could shoot," Peter insisted.

"I just can't," his father maintained. "I don't want to kill it."

Peter was in the car. All his friends' dads were getting deer, and coming home and bragging.

"Can't, can't—what do you mean? There's no such thing as can't. Shoot, shoot, shoot." Peter bounced up and down on the seat.

"No, I can't."

"Shoot it, Mom," Peter said.

"Do you want to shoot it?" his father asked his mother.

"Of course she does. Shoot it, Mom, shoot, for God's sake."

But before his father could pass the rifle over to his mother, the deer turned and hightailed it across the road, and without a sound it was gone.

"Well, there it goes," his father said. "It's gone now—good luck to it."

"What do you mean, 'good luck to it.' "

Peter told me that he knew his father was not going to be his inspiration as far as hunting and fishing went, so he began to hang out with his mother. She took him out fishing in the spring, and waded the brooks with him, and when Peter got a bit older she would drive him along the dirt roads as he hunted partridge. They would go along the road, in November, after a snowfall. It would be brilliantly cold at three in the afternoon and soon Peter would begin searching the trees.

"Stop"—and his mother would pull the car over. He would walk into the birches with his shotgun and come out a while later with a bird or two, and they would proceed on their way.

He became very good at doing this. He can spot a deer in

a chop-down quicker than anyone I know, or a salmon in a pool. It is as if he has a sixth sense about him.

One July, just after high school, he was on the south branch of the Sevogle for a fish, at Clearwater Pool. It was one of the few pools that he could drive to with his car. He had an old Hardy rod and reel, and a tapered leader to which he had attached a ten-pound test. I do not know if he still uses a tapered leader, but he did for years. Some friends of mine call tapered line a leftover from the years of gentleman trout fishing, but others swear by it, saying your fly will look more natural and move much better, and that your line lays out in a proper fashion. Besides this, it is easier to change a small leader if you get a knot or crimp when you have a tapered that stays on your main line.

This was the age when Peter began to fish bug—and now he has the best assortment of bugs of any man I know. They come in every size but they are slim and fast, usually with a little longer shank, tied back, for low water. He sometimes will use another fly, like a gull attracted to something bright, but not often—just as my friend David, from the Bartibog, will use almost anything *but* a bug.

Peter parked his car that long-ago day, took his Hardy rod and reel. He never bothered with his waders. He put on his vest and his Polaroid glasses, tied on a bug with brown hackle, and went down through Clearwater Pool, which had a bridge over it. The bridge is gone now, and so is the warden's camp that used to be there. I guess they were burnt. Clearwater is a nice, quiet pool that should hold fish, and though I've seen a fish or two taken from it, and hooked and landed fish there myself, it never seems as productive as it should be.

Peter didn't see anything at Clearwater that day either. And he was thinking that he would drive back around to Mullin Stream Bridge and walk from there into the Narrows Pool on the south branch of the Sevogle to fish—a good thirty-five-minute walk. But then with a spontaneity he has always had, he decided to walk the river.

"If I want to know where the pools are, then I must walk it."

And so he began an eight-mile journey on a river he had never been on before, with no one knowing where he was, to find pools he had never fished, sensing only that somewhere off to his right, over the great rugged hills of deep wood spruce, was an old logging road that would, if he could find it, lead him back to his car after dark. I suppose in a truly elemental way that day, years ago, was to become his baptism of fire.

It was a long walk, hugging one side of the river or the other, hanging on to branches to keep his balance, watching for sudden dips and pockets which would make him lose his balance. And after he got down about a mile he began to discover that this might not have been such a wise idea. It was like wading a part of the Amazon. Fishing was slow, and the water was low. The river, which empties into the big Sevogle, which in turn meets the Norwest Miramichi, is a very slippery one, so it's entirely possible to sprain or break an ankle from the rocks on the river or the hidden holes on the paths. And if you do this alone, miles from anywhere, you are in trouble. Especially when no one knows where you've gone to or where you are. And this was the situation he found himself in. Besides this, this baptism of fire—this elemental journey contains the blackfly and mosquito, bedded down and hatched by swamp ground on either side.

July is the best time for fishing the south branch, but that day he had yet to see a fish.

He walked down past the rough water of Simpson's Pool, down by Allie's Pool below it, and the river trailed away, spined and dotted by rocks, and interspersed with swift currents and small pockets, being swept by wind and bursts of rain. He got further down to a nice pool we were to call "Disappointment Pool" in the years to come, and continued on, past a large dead-water pool on his right, called "the Salmon Hole," where he was to take a beautiful salmon one day a few years later.

On the Sevogle the wind comes up suddenly and can interrupt or even ruin a good day, because you have a problem with casting and the fish don't want to take. A windy day for trout, Hemingway said, is a good day. As true as that might be, I don't know where the hell he was fishing. On the Miramichi the wind generally comes up some time about one in the afternoon, and might stay until evening, with the high banks on either side of these many fertile rivers acting as a wind tunnel.

Of all the rivers I have walked, and I have walked a good many, the south branch of the Sevogle is the worst. The river is spined with rocks, slippery and sharp, the bottom is uneven, flies are everywhere, and at certain places it's hard to keep your footing. Off on either side the footpaths are swallowed in thick branches and hidden holes. Off in the woods the ground is boggy and replete with mosquitoes.

It is a beautiful river, a habitat for moose and deer and bear, a picturesque place of startling grandeur and privacy, far away from man. It is where I have fished whole afternoons without seeing another soul, and brought fish back to our solitary camp at night. Very few rivers afford this.

About halfway on his journey down to Island Pool the day had cleared, and Peter was in a better mood. He had walked off his anxiety and was feeling in good shape. He relaxed a moment, studied the pool, and decided to give it a try.

Island Pool, he discovered, was not going to be an easy pool to fish because there was an undertow, where the small peninsula of land juts towards the right shore, and he found that at first his line just dragged in a swirling undertow. He then decided it was best to fish from the left bank because it was hard to work a fly on the right. But from that angle he knew he would miss what he thought was the hot spot in the deep agitated water at the top of the pool.

Still he went to the left and threw his fly towards the bottom of the pool, not thinking he would have any luck. This was an age ago now, and he was just beginning to know about where the fish might or might not lay. He was alone on the river, with miles more to go. On either side spruce and cedar ran up into high hills, which dwarfed him.

His fly—a bug with brown hackle—moved quickly, skimming the top of the water. But it skimmed the surface where the best part of the pool ended and flattened out into what seemed a dead shallow. He didn't think he was giving himself much of a chance at this pool and was looking downriver as he stripped his line, picked it up, and cast once more. You don't need a long line here, and he was just dabbing the water.

Then, as his bug lighted on the surface, he felt his line tighten and his rod began to bow.

He knew at once he had a big fish on. He didn't know then that fish would actually move out of a pool. He had not much idea about how strong an Atlantic salmon that has spent four years in the sea could be.

The salmon might have sensed this about him. For a moment it didn't do anything. It just sulked a bit, as he stood almost on top of it. And then he felt the reel begin to sing—*ZZzzzzZZZ*—and the fish began to move. More and more line went out, far into his backing. The day was clear, and the singing of the reel seemed to testify the beginning of a very private struggle. Then a fish jumped at the turn.

Another fish, he thought. And he realized in amazement that it was his fish. So trying to study the water beneath his feet, he began to move downriver towards it, trying to jump from rock to rock along the shore, reeling line in as he went. At times almost running. He and the fish seemed to be united not only in this struggle but in the fact that they were the only two creatures alive on this river.

Then he slipped and went down, and almost lost his rod. He got to his feet, and thought the fish was gone, only to suddenly feel the line tighten, the rod bow, and his line being taken out again.

He decided it was best to wade right across the river, to the other bank, for the fish had gone about a small bend on that side. At one point he found himself in water up to his chest and barely able to stay up.

The fish jumped again, but he managed to reach the other side; his rod, however, jutted out from a group of tangled thorns. And he knew there was positively no way he would be able to *beach* the fish from the side he was on. He was now about thirty feet from the fish, and holding it quite well, so he again started to cross the river—only to find, for some reason, that the fish started upriver when he did. When this happened his line was tangled around himself.

Here in water up to his waist, he had to hold the rod over his head, and turn counter-clockwise to free himself. When he got everything straightened out, the fish was still on.

He followed the fish back upriver, and came to a small beach, jutting a foot or so out from the bushes. The fish wasn't in a pool and there were rocks everywhere. At any given second he might snap his leader on a rock.

The fish was showing its back as it dug deep into its reserve and made its way out to the middle of the river, swirling the water away from it.

And then it began to run a little and turn on its stomach. So he knew it was spent. Once its nose was turned into shore, he backed right up against the side of the bushes and brought it in on a small landing.

He was exhausted. He was soaking and his arms ached. The fish was a male close to fifteen pounds. He had hooked in on a small bug at the lower end of the pool in about two and a half feet of water. There was still sea lice on it, and it had probably just come into the pool before he did. Perhaps as he had started his two-hour long trek down from Clearwater to Island Pool, it was making its way up past those rocks where he had played the life from it.

The day was starting to cloud, the water looked darker, and there was still a long way to go. The trees on either side of the river were silent, and thrust out to the sky in that self-absorbed way trees always have. He made his way, with his fish, downriver towards some place called White Birch he had not been to before. He carried the fish in one hand, the rod in the other, and tried to navigate the slippery stones, or along the paths that were overgrown with grass and alders.

He came to White Birch in the evening. The no-see-ums were at his hands and face, and every time he stopped mosquitoes flitted above him. But the pool, with its rock in the middle and its fine flow of dark water on the far side, was too inviting. He had to give it a try. Besides, he could easily cast and beach a fish here he decided.

He made a bed for his fish and walked up to the top of the pool and looked it over. It was an exceptionally fine pool.

Here you cast out to the far side letting your fly move towards the boulder that sits in the middle. The fish will lie behind that boulder, or just in front, but they will also lie between the boulder and the far cliff, nearer the top of the pool where the water enters the pool in a darkish-brown run.

It was prime time for fishing now and on the third cast he hooked a large grilse, just on the outside of the rock. The grilse swallowed the bug and jumped three times in succession, tired, and he landed it after a fifteen-minute fight. Then, with two fish, a rod, and no place to put them, he started up the hill, trying to find the path.

He looked here and there and began to cut up the side of the hill, and realized that though it may still be off-white on the late-evening water, it was already dark in the deep Sevogle wood.

It is a steep hill, the south branch of the Sevogle is a hard river to reach at any time, and as he kept going he felt he had missed the path, but he was also confident that he would find it again. Carrying two fish and a rod, and trying to get over windfalls as high as his waist or chest, with soaking wet jeans and slippery sneakers, was a hard enough venture. But he kept faith that off to his upper right was the old logging road that would walk him back to his car.

At certain points along the rise of the hill, it plateaus out for a few feet just to rise again. Here all kinds of small animals,, insects and plant life live out their lives in the warm summer air; squirrels and partridge, chipmunks and chickadees, constantly going about their business without ever caring or bothering about ours, and never understanding why we with chainsaws or oil and gas would bother them.

Trying to get up and down these hills is hard enough, but it's always worse when you don't have a bag to store your fish—and have no hands to keep the branches from your face. Your face can get torn up fairly badly if you aren't careful.

At one of these plateaus he stopped and looked about. It was boggy off to his right, but he felt the road had to be in that direction. Only the sky held a shaft of fading light. The wood itself was dark. He knew he didn't want to twist an ankle in here.

He didn't get too many feet until he came to a giant windfall just over waist high. He managed to sit upon it, looking back towards the direction he had come in, still hearing the river faintly, and heaved himself over it. It was a three-foot drop on the other side into a dark undergrowth. And he fell headlong into it, fish and rod in hand, onto the stomach of a giant black bear.

"It gave me a fright," he said.

The bear had crawled up in there to die some time that spring, far away from the tracks of man, thinking never to be found.

Later, and in almost ink dark, Peter made it out to the logging road, both fish in tow, and walked the eight miles back to his car.

We ran the Norwest with canoe twice my first summer. We usually ran the river after a rain, and with the water dropping. With the water dropping the fish would take, the grassy banks seemed more fertile, and the runoffs propelled twigs and leaves into the water. But the more the water dropped, the more it cleared. By mid-morning the sky would be hot enough, tempered with small distant clouds. The flies were ferocious, and made me think of writing a song to them. There is a song called "The Little Blackfly." There is also a poem about blackflies by Alden Nowlan. Nowlan describes hating them so much it almost turns to love.

On my first canoe trip I hooked a grilse above Wilson's Pool on a Red Butt Butterfly. I was with Fred Irving. He pointed to a small run and said, "Throw your fly there."

I did—and *bang*.

But I lost it because I was overanxious. That is, I tried to pull the fish into shore and turned away from it when it jumped. It wasn't that well hooked but hooked well enough to land if I'd had the patience and experience. When the line went slack I felt for the first time that inescapable loss mixed with old and ancient desire. Tolstoy's character Dolohov in *War and Peace* once said about bear hunting: "Sure, everyone's afraid of a bear—but once you set eyes on him your only fear is that he'll get away!"

Everyone might feel empathy for the salmon as well, but when you hook one you have this desire to never lose it.

Later that month Peter and I took a tent with us. We camped halfway along the Norwest run, at Cedar Pool, and pitched a tent in the dark. We were both sunburnt and tired. We had been on the river many days at that time. I had even had a fish or two to show for it. We cooked up supper in silence and crawled into the tent, assuring ourselves that the first light would wake us, and we'd be in the pool before anyone else. Our rods were ready to go as we drifted off to sleep.

We were awakened by shouts of excitement.

We sleepily got up and went outside. Already the morning was warm, and three people were in the pool, with two more canoes parked on either side of our tent. A woman of about forty-five had a fish on, and was playing it at the lower part of the pool. The other two people had already taken fish, which rested in the fish bed they had made. One was a salmon about ten pounds, the other a grilse. The woman had watched the fish come for the fly once, rested it, and threw back to it again.

They picked up their fish and congratulated each other. Then nodding to us, packing their fish in the canoes, they headed downriver.

"Nice morning," Peter managed.

The pool was dead after that, even though we had it all to ourselves. And we packed up and went back up in the afternoon. We came to a camp that overlooked the river. It flowed below us, as Peter sat on an old couch and spoke to me about his working the pool. It would be better to throw a line as close to the bank as possible. He pointed to a rip, three-quarters of the way down, and told me he had seen a fish there. I could see nothing, though I looked for ten minutes.

As he spoke, unknown to him, a mouse scampered out of the couch and climbed up on his shoulder, listening to his story.

Later he went down and crossed the river, and began to fish through. I had a good vantage point where I could see how his fly moved over every inch of water. He threw it exactly where he wanted. Suddenly in that dark rip, three-quarters of the way through the pool, he hooked a fish.

"I figured it was there," he said.

For the next month or so I travelled miles of water, and seemed to get worse every time I went out. Nothing worked to my advantage, because I couldn't use my left hand effectively enough to strip line, and when I cast the line itself would bunch up at the first eye of the rod. My left hand was my great deterrent. I decided it might be better if I cut it off. I seriously thought about it on more than one occasion those first few summers. I had a good knife, and though I never actually did cut my hand off, my left hand got in the way so much I had on more than one occasion given myself some serious injuries. For instance, I couldn't open a door with my left hand, or button a shirt button, or pick up a cup of coffee. So it was certainly not earning its keep. About the only thing it was good for was getting my line tangled up in it.

Once as a boy I had cut my left hand to the bone, trying to build a camp. I went to the first house I came to, looking for first aid. A nice lady opened the door, looked at me, shrieked, slammed the door and locked it.

"It's only a little blood—scaredy cat," I managed. I went about the windows of the house, holding my hand out, touching the panes of glass, and smearing all her windows with blood in an effort to show her how harmless I was. Sometimes I would reach a certain window before she came into that room, always with a slight acrimonious smile on my face.

Finally I had to make my way home alone.

At any rate, I left the hand exactly where it was for the time being, dangling down somewhere, and got on without it. I tried to strip line leaving it in the water, but that was as ineffective as anything else. Once doing this I picked up the line, the fly came catapulting back and hit me in the eye. So I walked about with a black eye for three days.

"How did you get the black eye?"

"Fishing."

"Sure. Fishing. How in God's name can you get a black eye fishing?"

"You have to work at it, but it can be done," I maintained.

But then, that was my arm. I could write a book about my feet. Often at night, back home, far from the river, I would have to soak my left foot in a tub to get it moving again for the next day. I would bend over and slap at my toes to see if they still worked. I would pry them apart, try to wiggle them. I have the problem of instant arthritis, and sometimes coming out of a pool I would sit on the bank for an hour because my left foot was so sore. Once or twice I would go crawling about on the beach as if I had been shot at by a sniper and was trying to find cover.

So that play-acting with Mr. Simms about my left foot aching came back to haunt me.

Everyone has their problems and this was, and is, mine. I am making no more of it than a man of conscience or integrity should. But I will never lessen the effect upon me over the years. I will never say that it didn't affect me to be polite to those who have no knowledge of its effect. I will only say I was born with it, and can do nothing about it. Nor would I change it now, even if I could. It is not bragging when I say that for me to have two good arms seems entirely like cheating.

As I grew older I became more and more determined to do whatever I wanted to do and now look upon it as an obligatory challenge. And an obligatory challenge means exactly what it implies: You suffer the aches and pains and ridicule along the way.

If I have no balance, which is dangerous when you are crossing a swift river in waders, I would forgo the waders. I would cross the river anyway. People who know me have seen me do this time and again, without any comment about it. Besides, I rationalized that water was only cold in early June—by mid-June I didn't need them. I've gone down in waders before—once when I was crossing the Norwest Miramichi alone. All of a sudden my feet were bobbing along like buoys and my head was slapping the rocks.

It was not that much fun, but I did manage to pull myself out.

One morning Peter decided to take the day off work.

The river was just the right level, and filled with fish. It was early July, dark and fertile pools were the right temperature, the water was lowering after a night's rain, and *he* hooked fish all day. Finally disgusted that he was hooking so many, and *me* none at all, he crossed the river and climbed a tree that tiered over the far bank in the shimmering summer air. I hadn't a clue what he was doing, but I watched him as if I did. Every now and then I'd wave, just to pretend I knew exactly why he was thirty feet in the air.

He crawled way out on a limb, which sagged with his weight, and looking down at the pool he began pointing out fish to me.

"There," he said. "There, there, there, and there," he said, pointing at grilse lying in the run out from me, as if he was tapping with one finger on a giant fish tank. But even so, I couldn't make them come for my fly. Peter mumbled something, I don't know what, but I think it was: "David—are you brain dead?"

And then: "Oh, a salmon—he's coming—he's coming—he's—stopped. Throw your fly over him again."

Which I duly did.

"Oh—here he comes. He's coming—he's coming. He—oh—he stopped."

This went on for the better part of an hour. Finally Peter crawled back down the tree and crossed the river, totally compressed. He picked up his rod on the far bank, and with his fly dangling haphazardly above the funnel of water at the bottom of the pool he started to cross the river again. To my astonishment and his, a grilse leapt right up out of the water and grabbed his dangling fly. He played it behind his back, as if he was wrestling with an invisible growth on his shoulder.

Finally he landed it, playing it behind him all the while, and picked it up, looked at it, and threw it back.

He began to mumble again, mumbling and mumbling away to himself. I think in a certain way he felt embarrassed. I know I did.

After that day, I began to question everything. My line was too visible. Fish could make out my line—or they could see my boots. Fish could hear me, when they couldn't hear anyone else. I would have to sneak up on them. I would have to come at them some different way. While other people just walked to the river, I would have to fall to my knees and crawl behind them through the woods.

I kept changing flies after every few casts. I became suspicious of the fish. The fish knew who I was. I'd have to camouflage my feet—so they wouldn't think I was me.

There is a psychology to this of course and I am not the only beginner to have experienced it. It is quite simple and therefore remarkable, and it is a mental catch-22. In order to have the confidence to catch fish, you must have caught fish before. If you keep fishing without luck, then you are bound to lose this confidence, and once this is gone, nothing seems to work. This is the experience in every sport, and it is the same in fishing. So not only did my ability, such as it was, to catch fish diminish, my ability to cast, to read the water, to work a pool all suffered. And was to suffer for the better part of the first two summers. The statement that nothing succeeds like success is true.

I had yet to experience this rather remarkable indication of expertise. When I found it in later years, I too felt I could take a fish in any pool given a chance. But it was an apprenticeship that most fishermen go through.

I had, in fact, without realizing it, learned a great deal. I had learned where a fly would work and how a fish would show for a bug, how to cast a dry fly, and something about the water level and the fish's desire to take. I knew about the chance you'd have in high water, or water dropping, or the time of day. I always remembered where a fish took, who took it, and what fly they were using.

Later that summer we walked the south branch of the Sevogle every day. On it, there was a nice little run above Three Minute Pool (a pool we'd reach after a forty-five-minute walk over large boulders and stingers), and I decided to try it our last day fishing that year. I crossed the river in the rapids and walked up above the run, threw my line across, watched the fly work in the nice current, and realized I was casting for the first time not too badly. I had on a Copper Killer—a fly I always loved, and have put on at least once a fishing trip ever since.

I worked my way down the meandering run, and a fish boiled for my fly. I rested it and worked towards it again. About two or three feet from the far bank, the fish, a grilse, took. I knew he was well hooked, and I knew I wouldn't lose this fish. I didn't. I also suddenly realized that once I began to fish alone, and travel the rivers by myself, I would gain confidence and have better luck. And I did.

Seven

EARLY IN THE SEASON of my third year I went down to Dave Savage's to get some flies. He was sitting in his shed, alone. Across in the dooryard he had his large canoe on the trailer ready to go to the Restigouche, a red flag tied to the stern. His outboard motor, gas can and a poling pole were sitting upon the lawn. Evening was coming on, and the road was silent. Far away you could hear mothers calling out to their children, while below the Miramichi flowed out towards the bay, in a way that melted water and horizon in the far-off distance. A buoy light twinkled and everything was still.

Savage was tying up flies to take with him. They were in part some of the same flies he would fish with on the Miramichi but he put a double barb on some, like the Black Dose, the White Ghost, Blue Charm, and he gave me a Black Dose to put into my box.

As I stood there, near a hundred new flies, a dozen plumbed feathers, the last of the quiet evening sun came through the door's window.

I helped him load the equipment into the trailer. In the clear clean midsummer air he spoke fondly about the Restigouche, the only river he considers a match to the Miramichi.

He came back from the Restigouche with a thirty-three-pound salmon, as my older brother and I prepared to go.

We went there in late July of that year, by ourselves, in a small canoe with a motor that didn't work well. It was large water, and wonderful huge pools, but we needed a much bigger canoe. Its ratio of big salmon to grilse was about three to one; just the reverse of the Miramichi. But this was our first try at it and we had to learn as we went, so to speak. On the Restigouche one fishes from the relative comfort of a canoe. You start at the top of a pool, cover the water your cast will allow you to reach, then drop down a canoe length, drop anchor, and start the process again. Sooner or later you will have covered all your water, and if lucky, have a fish or two to show for it.

By the time we got packed into the camp, after running the canoe eight miles or so, it was supper hour. It was a glorious night, the camp was nestled in the hills and the river flowed beneath us, a canopy of stars and shooting stars over our head.

Camps of course are always centres for nostalgia. And there are many reasons for it. The air drifts through patches of board and mattress that have been there thirty years, the men and women have come and gone. Whole lives are lived out in moments of exhilaration, in showing off flies that took a certain fish, or the way in which a fish was lost, after fighting you for thirty minutes. The camps will wait, and come alive again only when someone is in them. That is when the memory of the fish comes alive also. Camps generously hold the memories and ghosts of others. Of other fish, of other days gone away. These memories, reminiscences, come alive in the glow of the propane lanterns, just at the edge of the corners.

So fishing camps force themselves upon you, and become a place and a time for reverie and a certain spiritual readjustment. Those people who might never believe in a religious retreat will retreat to these camps deep in the woods near a living river, feeling the grace of the sun, seeing wondrous splendid stars, and, even if it is unconscious, re-examining their lives. For here is another life, not only the life of the fly and the rod, but a life that says that so much of our concerns—which we put so much stock in and trouble ourselves so much about—does not matter in the least. We have too much, we fret too much, we hoard away too much for ourselves. These camps can and always do tell us this if we listen to them and the water running below them. That human kindness matters, and companionship, and our love of and protection for those who are far away from us at that moment, but not much else.

In the camp pool that first evening I hit a salmon but couldn't keep it on. I saw its enormous belly roll over my fly as it tightened the line, before my leader went limp. But it was a great thrill, although I had caught two salmon the year before; I don't think either of them went half that size. So it would have been a tough fight. Sometimes you present the fly in a wrong way for a fish to take well, but present it well enough for a fish to show or *touch.* Often the fish won't come back. That night it didn't though I fished over it for a long time, cursing myself for what I might have done wrong.

The next day we were up early and out on the river. We got up at dawn, and spent most of the warm, clear day on the river. We travelled back and forth from one pool to the other, until our arms ached from casting. But unfortunately the motor we had gave us problems the entire time, especially travelling up against the current. At some places we would have to get out, and tinker with the engine at the water's edge for an hour at a time. The river is wide, and the pools are large. If you are on your own the first time, it takes you a while to read them. If your motor is no good, you're in a worse bind.

So we did not have much success. Late on the second day my brother took off his pants, got out of the canoe, and waded the river. He found a small run about a mile below the camp that we hadn't bothered with. He put on a butterfly. I sat watching him from the canoe, chewing tobacco and having a tea. (You can do both at the same time if you're careful.) Suddenly I saw this huge shape come from a lay towards his little fly skittering across the run.

When the salmon did take, an instant later, it almost tore the rod from his hand. It took him forty-five minutes to land. He was dead tired at the end of it. But one thirty-pound salmon made it a grand day.

As he was playing it, wearing fishing vest and underwear, two canoes stopped to take pictures.

In the camp on the Restigouche later that second night, after supper was over and I was outside chewing some tobacco, I thought of my uncles and my grandmother. The night was soft and warm. We had befriended the camp squirrel who would come down the spruce tree and wait on the bottom porch step for pieces of bread. This was where half of my life was from—my uncles and aunts.

It seemed, however, that their lives were so removed from mine. They grew up in a much harsher environment. In the 1930s, things were much different on the river. The guides, for instance, who all seemed to wear ties, erectly posed in the old pictures I have seen. But it was always a harder and more uncomfortable journey for the sport.

This environment has changed considerably and with it the rivers. The woods might be still deep or dark, but the journey into those woods is accommodating. When my uncles had to walk for miles through those woods, now a half-ton makes it in an hour or two. The land has been muted and stilled.

I remembered my grandmother into her early nineties, the first time I took my wife to meet her. She came into the dooryard and grabbed my arms in hers, and shook them with her still strong hands, a kinsman of her blood. It was the last time I was to see her.

She told me that she had never been to a circus or a dance. My mother's family never spoke about their past. But it would come back in glimpses as I spoke with this frail, still active woman. Her sons, one died when he was a child, all went to work in the woods when they were little more than children themselves, and guided the American and Canadian sports.

Back in my youth I would hear the stories of fishing at the table in the afternoons from uncles who came now and then from the great green-watered Matapedia, and fished and guided the sports along those sweeping rivers long ago, in large twenty-four-foot cedar canoes, with poles. This was far, far back in the 1950s when I was a child and the country was still innocent and ignorant, about what our resources were and what we could do with them. And the men who came to fish would look at those guides, I suppose, as hewers of wood and drawers of water. And many of these guides were my uncles.

Sometimes when I see old documentary films about fishing on the Miramichi, I can relate them to old documentary films I've seen about fishing on the Amazon, or game hunting in Africa. They sometimes have the same flavour about them. Some of the men my uncles guided were essentially like Teddy Roosevelt shooting the rhino and the lions on his eighteen-month safari through Africa, with African guides, living off the land in tents. Like Africans, we were always in some way part of someone else's hinterland. That, in a way, is our life as rural

Canadians. But even if that is so, let us not be scornful of it or diminish its worth.

The Teddy Roosevelts of the world continue to come here, like a man I once met in Montreal, not without the indecent naiveté to expect too much from the land we offer, completely, without knowing at times what it is truly worth.

This was my reverie that night. But it was not harsh. It was a reverie tinged with a sad kindness. The Congo, the Nile, the Amazon, the Miramichi. One is not more peculiar than the other to the imagination of men living in the Midwestern cities, or in New York, or walking in the evening to some out-of-date empire club.

Men, similar to Mr. Roosevelt, men like the great sharpshooter, Mr. Boa, came here for caribou and moose. And they came here to fish as well. I suppose the guides they had might have acted out a part for them similar to the part Mr. Roosevelt's guides did. Always with smiles and running about to make sure things were done well. (This is never to deny Mr. Roosevelt's greatness as an adventurer or his boundless courage.)

Yet there is something that would always separate the guide from the sport. Sometimes it was as different as life knowledge compared to acquired taste.

And that is the indigenous quality of the Miramichi and

its guides. They take these sports to places the sports have never been in search of those fish that those sports remember they have searched for as far back as the Mother Goose stories of their childhood. It becomes in part a certain longing to make good on the promises you made to yourself as a child. And I thought of this as I fed the little squirrel its bread.

Once one of my uncles, at the age of seventeen, was walking into a camp one day in midwinter. He was travelling with an older man, who became tired halfway along on their journey, on this cold day in January of 1935. My uncle built a fire and tried to warm him, and get him moving again, but, as the afternoon wore on, it was to no avail.

"You go ahead," the older man said. "I'm 'bout done."

"You'll freeze in the night before we can get back to you," my uncle said. The wind had come up strong and there was a palpable taste to the air.

But the older man said he was unable to walk. That his legs had given out.

"I did the only thing I could," my uncle said.

"What was that?"

"I carried him."

My grandmother, who cooked for sports and men all her life, would never have expected anything less.

I do not know which uncle was the greatest in the woods, nor would I make it a contest, but one, Richard Adams, became world famous as a guide. The most famous people he guided were Jimmy Carter and his wife Rosalind. When Rosalind took a salmon that day they asked my uncle how much it weighed. He glanced at it—"Twenty-eight and a half pounds," he said.

When they weighed it the scales said: twenty-eight and three-quarters.

He is a frail older man now, but until last summer he was still guiding and doing things, which he said you couldn't learn in a book.

That was my reverie, my source of reaffirmation, that night on the Restigouche. The little squirrel went home to bed, the propane light in the cabin flared out into the dark, the river ran on.

The sports have their own stories; the guides have theirs. Sometimes on a hard day, it is harder on the guide than on the fisherman. The guide will begin to hate the river he loved for so long. If the fisherman is cranky or unsatisfied, and if the guide is conscientious, it is a hard go.

Sometimes the guide will have to listen over and over again to the same hopes in stories told by people who believe in the esotericness of fly-fishing, without understanding much more of it than that.

The meandering river, the sun just behind the trees, the fly dropped perfectly just at the right point in the pool, the line laid out so softly it gives a beat to the heart, and then from deep under the water in a hidden lay, a swirl and the line tightening. The guide knows this but still it is hard for him or her at times to act enthusiastically after forty straight days, rain and shine, on the river.

Sometimes a guide will tell a fisherman he has seen a fish rise, just to keep interest alive.

"You just raised a fish," he will say. Sometimes a fisherman might know this isn't true but hope keeps him silent. Or they will talk about how fishing was the week before. Or how it will be better the next day. Fishing can break your heart if you are between the good days. And this is how you can generally gauge things. If you get into a camp late at night, and people are talking about how well fishing had gone the week before, you are almost certain that fishing is going to be hard and slow.

Some guides will do anything to get his sport a fish. My uncle carried people on his back across rivers to afford them the best opportunity to fish a pool. He made sure they were not only in the best position to fish, but he made sure that they had on the best fly to allow a chance. If a guide is conscientious, things are done to make a sport feel at home but never incompetent. They know that it is their world and the sport at times is out of place in it. A guide knows in a second what calibre the fisherman is, and how to adjust his day about that unspoken qualification.

One day I was fishing private water on the main Souwest with a guide and a person from Calgary. The guide had gotten a little disgusted with fishing. He almost declared that there were no fish.

Though he didn't say it quite this way he still had that look about him that made you feel wetting a line was a terrible imposition on himself.

I was at a camp with a contingent of other fishermen, most of them clients of lawyers, who were being given a kind of trip of a lifetime because of what their lawyers had billed them. There were six guides. I arrived just before supper. I was told there had not been a fish taken in three days, and everyone was just a little tired. So of course it became a trip that soon had nothing to do with fishing for many of these people, who had a good supply of booze on hand. They were ridden in a canoe, by a guide, where they would drink, and if inclination allowed, throw a fly or two at some water.

After supper, at about five in the afternoon, I met my

guide. He had retired from his work in town, was now guiding in the summer and fall, and spent winter on unemployment insurance.

"Will we see a fish?" I said good naturedly as I shook hands.

"God knows," he said. "There hasn't been any seen in days—last week was great—but the water is low, and we need a rain."

I knew we needed a rain, but still and all, the water level didn't look so bad—and I felt that a fish would take if you could position a fly over it.

"I just finished three days of hard fishing without anyone taking a fish," he said, and he screwed up his eyes at me.

"That's too bad," I shrugged. And I looked at my partner, a young man from Calgary who hadn't fished before. I felt a little sad for him, standing as he was in his brand-new everything and waiting to be told where to go and what to do. It reminded me of myself not so many years before.

The young man from Calgary was very uninformed about fishing—and therefore very informed in the wrong way. He worried constantly.

"What will we do if we see a bear?" he asked, half in bravado and half in fear.

"Run a mile, shit a pile, and hide behind it," the guide said lackadaisically. Which did nothing to lessen the man's worry.

I too had been worried about bears in the woods until I met a few and saw them. It is still true, as it was with my dog Jeb Stuart and I, that almost none of them will bother anyone, and will turn and be long gone before you can ever get a good look at them. This was just as true on the Norwest one day when I saw a bear swimming the river. The bear crossed the river not many yards from me, went over to my truck, sniffed it, and hightailed it away faster than I have ever seen. But still I wouldn't want to startle one on a path somewhere with a cub, as Jeb and I did, again.

It was late in August and after six in the afternoon when we finally stepped into the canoe, the guide pulled the cord, the outboard started, and away we went, downriver towards a small island that had a pool on the far side of it. We pulled into the island and walked down to the water. The water was flowing along. A few feet out from the bar there was a constant swift ripple that lasted for about twenty yards. Just on the outside of that rip you could see where the deeper water joined, and anywhere along there fish would be laying.

"Get into her," the guide said, sitting in the canoe, and swatting at flies with his hat.

"Where do I fish?" the man from Calgary said.

"Walk along the bar—" the guide pointed. "And when you get up to the top throw your line over—and fish down through."

The man from Calgary looked uncertain. He stepped into the water up to his knees and looked behind him.

"Keep going," the guide said.

He stepped further along and looked back again. "What will I do if I fall in?" the man from Calgary said. "You'll be able to get me out—with these waders on, eh?" he asked.

"Just make sure your hat floats so we know where your body is," the guide said.

The man looked plaintively back at me and blinked two big sad blinks, as if this fishing trip of a lifetime was a fishing trip from hell, and stood exactly where he was, dabbing his line before him as if he was searching for minnows. I waited for him to move along through the pool, and he didn't. I didn't want to go in front of him, didn't want to go above him and not be able to throw my line, so after waiting for ten minutes I began to look about for an alternative place to fish.

I spied a stretch across the river and down below us about three hundred yards.

"Is that on our stretch?" I said, pointing.

"That's the end of her," the guide said.

"Well, I'm going to wade across and fish there," I said. "Is it any good?"

"Oh, ya get at her," the guide said, grinning, not even trying to hide his disdain at my question.

I was starting to dislike him. I disliked him because he felt he was competent and we were not. But no one I've ever respected takes pride in lessening another man or woman because of their own capability, and I was awash in sympathy for my young friend from Calgary.

I crossed the river and made my way along the tangled sloping bank on the far side. Old growth woods loomed off to my left, and as I walked the bank became steeper and steeper, so that I ended up wading along the river to the stretch I had seen.

There was another canoe below me about four hundred yards, with two sports fishing from it, and my own guide sat in the stern of the canoe, waving at flies. I looked back, and my young acquaintance from Calgary had come out of the water and was offering him a beer. So with beers in hand they both stood by the canoe, drinking.

I went to the top of the water. It wasn't half as good as the stretch I had left. The water was slow and dark. About twenty yards out from me there was a rock with another smaller rock just up to its right, and I felt that just between those rocks, on the far side, was the prime place for a fish to lay. I began working my way along to it, using a Green Butt Butterfly, because it seemed to me like butterfly country. On about the fifth or sixth cast, just before I reached the rocks, I had a grilse on. At that position my back was slightly turned to my guide.

There was absolutely no place to beach the fish, unless I wanted to haul it right up the sheer bank on my left. The guide had the net. I waved at him, but he wasn't looking my way. And so I played the fish. The grilse gave a run, and jumped twice, and looked like it had been in the river for a while. I turned and called out to the guide. No response. And then knowing the grilse was spent, I looked about for a place to beach it.

Up the sheer bank on my left was where I could go. I yelled to my guide again. No response again. But by this time, the canoe on the stretch below me was lifting anchor to come to my aid with a net.

At about this time my guide looked up, saw the bow in my line, and the grilse make another small leap, and frantically became interested in my position. He pushed the canoe out and began to pole downriver towards me, yelling, "Wait on it—wait on it."

But I decided then and there I was going to gain or lose this fish without his support. So turning the grilse towards shore, and measuring how far up the bank I would be able to scamper without falling over backwards, up I went. The grilse came behind me. And I was able to drop my rod and pick it up, kill it. I was scraping the scales from it when my guide arrived.

The next morning I got a grilse early, on another stretch of water above the camp, but that was all that was taken when I was there. Our guide had changed radically. He kept asking if we needed anything, and it was never a bother to fish with people who knew what they were doing. I thought of the little grilse I had taken and wondered if they knew anything of what their lives played in what just went on.

ONE SUMMER, BACK IN the early eighties, I fished mostly with Alvin Simms. He could no longer drive for his eyes were bad, and so I took him out.

We would go out early—sometimes getting on the river by five o'clock, me driving my old Suzuki Jeep. As June gave way to July we switched rivers, as July gave way to August we switched again, and each switch fulfilled a certain destiny for a certain number of fish.

Mr. Simms was a great caster, and always took more fish than I. He was as unconsciously a part of the river as any man

I have ever fished with. The best of it was, like all men I have fished with who are comfortable with themselves, he expected nothing from you.

Going down the Norwest in a canoe with him, he would pole to a dead still at the upper edge of a rapid, which would afford me time, at leisure to fish over a promising stretch or rock.

"There's a fish there," he whispered to me one morning, just below Stickney Pool, where the salmon always hold hard to the left bank before they enter Stickney itself. It is a deep leisurely part of the river between Stickney and the flat above Cedar Pool. I had often seen fish take here, and I believed him, but for the life of me, I couldn't budge a fish or make one show. And by this time I had taken fish.

"Change flies," he whispered urgently. "Put on that Bear Hair you have." Which showed that even though his eyes were poor, just by a glance he knew the flies I had.

I did and I fished. Let my line follow the angle over the huge rocks beneath the run, watching the little blackfly move, waiting at every second with an anticipation that Mr. Simms had produced in me. The fly moved in the current towards the fish.

"Now," he said.

And I tensed. But the fly moved across that clean water in the sun and wasn't disturbed along the three-inch spot we were both watching.

"Ah," he said, spitting, and holding the canoe fast with the pole. "Try 'er again, Davy. Jot yer fly over it, move it a little."

I flubbed the cast. He waited. I began to get anxious. To jot my fly would be a new experience though I wasn't skeptical that was what was needed. I brought the rod back, checked my leader, looked over at him.

"Try 'er again, she's there." He whispered in the urgent way a guide does early in the morning. The sun warmed his old sweater and touched the peak of his cap. His face, looking at the water, was as captivated as a child's.

I threw a better cast this time at forty-five degrees above the fish. The fly would come right over its nose, I felt. The line went out, and the fly floated down and touched the current. My fly began to arc. I watched it. There is a point when you know the fish must take—right NOW. I tried to jot it as Mr. Simms asked. But all I managed to do was make a ripple. The fly went past that point by a centimetre, then two, then a foot, then two.

"Must be me," I said.

"Try 'er again," he said. There was not a breeze in the air, no other fisherman in sight. Only the sound of the rapid above us and the occasional knock of the pole against the gunnel of the canoe.

I tried twice more. Both times we waited, watched the fly

skirt over the hidden rock, move away from the dark spot on the rock's far side we were both watching in anticipation.

"Give 'er here," he said.

I handed the rod to him. He braced the pole, took the rod in the other hand, holding the canoe fast in the water, and threw the line. It went towards the rock. He moved his wrist back and forth, the line trembled, the fly looked like it was jumping up and down on the water. The fly dotted along for a second, two seconds, three—*bang*. The rod bowed, the line began to zing from the pull of a young salmon.

"Here you go," he said. "I'll pole it in."

I might say that sometimes that works and a lot of times it doesn't. In fact, I watched him try it again a few times after this with no success at all. The truth remains, if a fish is going to take, it will take.

As we sat on the shore, he made up tea with seven bags in a two-cup pot, stirring it with a stick. And then later we poled back into the rapids and moved downriver.

He was growing old, and the world was changing. He was well over sixty that summer. He had an old camp, with an old flat-iron stove and three cots. He had a pin-up picture of a young woman selling lubricant from the late fifties, dressed in Levi's shorts and a halter top. He had some rods on the walls, a trophy or two, his diary. If he was there when you went to his camp, the door was always opened. No one bothered him. He would walk over the hill to his own little stretch and fish. It wasn't a great pool, but like so many home pools, once a person became familiar with it, knew where the fish were and had some luck, it became a place to invest their time. And he knew his old pool very well.

The problem was, that year he was told by people from away that he no longer could fish it. They put up a sign near the water, and met him on the shore three times to tell him he wasn't welcome. This happened quickly and without warning. And I still don't know the full extent of it. But he did not happen to have riparian rights to the water. The camp that did—a mile or so below him—had decided that he was a bother to them and to their camp guests.

For a while he put up a fight, said he'd get proof and no one could fool him. Said he would rock the pool or fill it all in. But he could no more do that than hurt someone. Then there were lawyers and all the rest of it involved. He told me that everyone had decided it wasn't him but a Mr. Jeffreys from Halifax who owned the water. He said he would build another camp somewhere—even though this one was forty years old. He looked about, saw others fishing on the water he once considered his, water which he never tried to regulate himself, and asked me to drive him to the south branch.

So I did. We got into the Jeep one morning and went around the Fraser Burchill Highway to the south branch of the Sevogle on a day in late July. He sat in the Jeep with his hands folded, looking out the window, looking like a child who has just been punished.

"I'll show you a place to fish," he said. "It's where I'll build me new camp. I'll go over to Fred-ric-ten—that's what I'll do—I'll go to Fred-ric-ten, and talk to the Forestry."

I took a road beyond Clearwater Pool, came to the top of a hill. We both looked down, where far, far away the river turned into the sun.

For miles there wasn't a tree. The ghostly remnants of trees stood in single file, blackened and desperate against the yellowish horizon. Like the rainforest, like all those things man had come to take for granted, to step upon, it had been clear-cut out. Old Mr. Simms had not been there in years. His lips trembled just slightly, the river in the distance glittered like a bayonet affixed against the sky.

"I'm a fool," he said.

"NO, yer not," I said.

"I got no place to fish now." He smiled, shaking his head.

The next Saturday I went to his camp. However, this time, the door was closed.

Nine

BY THE END OF THE sixth summer I had managed to learn to fish. And I fished mostly alone, leaving the cottage where Peg and I lived in the summer at dawn and trying to get back by mid-afternoon. I always carried with me, besides my dog, two rods, two reels weighted with weight-forward lines for those rods, three boxes of flies—bugs and butterflies being my favourite—a flashlight, a spare pair of jeans, and waders, two jugs of water (for the radiator), a thermos of tea, and a lunch bucket of sandwiches.

I love travelling the rivers alone, and now spend much more

time by myself than with other people, even though I'll never forget them for teaching me what they could.

By then, my line was touching the water where I wanted it to and I was able to cover the water I wanted to as well. (But I still got knots and flubbed casts and had days when nothing went right.) I no longer used a blood knot, but went with nine or ten feet of leader. I was using both hands, without having to think about it, and felt comfortable whenever I went fishing.

Often I did not make it back by afternoon. It would be dark when I left in the morning and dark when I got back out at nightfall. I stood in pools in the pouring rain, too stupid to come out of them, and I wallowed about the shore in the desperate fly-soaked heat too stupid to go home. And more than once I had to rely on luck to get my old truck started, miles away from anyone.

Some days I would start into Little River Pool just above the Miner's Bridge on the Norwest, but go on the long rough road into B&L.

The year before, Peter had seen a grilse jump in the swift little run, directly off from where the path came out unto the shore—on the other side of the river, and he left B&L Pool one day and went down and hooked two grilse. Although most people bypassed this run, which ran tight to the other shore between two rocks, grilse always rested there on their journey before moving into the pool proper. Or they would rest there and move right through the pool. So we usually stopped to throw a line over it. It was easy to reach. One just walked out up to their knees and threw a short tight cast into the top of the run, defined by an eddy swirling over a submerged rock. From there to another rock half-submerged about thirty yards downriver, it was a run alive with possibilities.

This run below B&L didn't look like much but it was often as not productive—until about eleven-thirty in the morning, when the action would taper off. It fished better in the morning than in the evening, and you could take fish on a variety of flies. I fished bug on the Norwest. But I've taken grilse on butterfly and Black Ghost, and Blue Charm, there as well.

One day that year I took my younger brother John and another man into B&L. My brother just came along for the ride, which was so bumpy the other man said he would never travel with me again—and so I've not invited him.

It was a nice day in early July and we walked down the long sun-drenched path to the water. Our acquaintance turned to his right and headed for the pool, about a quarter of a mile away.

"I'm fishing here," I said to my brother.

John looked at the water as I waded out up to my knees.

"The pool's up that way," he said.

"I know," I said.

"Well, why are you fishing here? There's no water here."

"Oh, there is fish here," I said, although I was unsure of it at that moment.

"Where?" John said, craning his neck and looking at me in a kind of embarrassment.

"Right here," I said. My little brown hackled bug landed on the far side of the flat rock and the line tightened. It was the first and probably only time I was able to predict a fish would take at the very instant it did.

In July we moved on to the Little Souwest—which is perhaps my favourite of all rivers and fishes well all July. The fish on the Little Souwest seemed to be always slightly brighter and more active to me than those on the Norwest. It is a bigger and in some ways grander river with less pressure on it than the Norwest. But the fish came in spurts because of the nets from the reserve just below.

It was on the Little Souwest where I decided one day that year to give up waders as soon as it got warm. It is a larger river with many tricky spots, and I was there one afternoon with David Savage. We were crossing in high water to Clellend Pool, and I was almost halfway across when I realized I had no left leg under me whatsoever. I let out my fishing line for balance, but knew that I could not go back or forth. There I was. The water swelled about me in the middle of the river. I tried to take one more step, and started to go, on the slippery boulders beneath me. Just below me the pool gleamed in the morning sunshine. But I wouldn't be able to stop from being swept into the rapids beyond them.

I hated to call out to anyone but I knew I would have to. And back Savage came and helped me across. It was a great day to fish, so I'm happy I didn't miss it. After that day, as soon as it got warm at all, my waders were relegated to the back of the truck.

The next day I was again fishing with David Savage. We both caught grilse very early in the morning. By afternoon the river seemed dead. But hour after hour David kept at it. He would sit on the log on the beach, stare at the water like a man investigating a certain painting for the tell-tale signature stroke of the painter, take a chew of plug, stare at the beach, and look through his box, swatting flies away with his hand. And then he would go out into the pool again and fish. It was a long pool, and had three different sections to it. The pool far at the top of the island we were on was deep and had two swift-running rips, which joined in a *Y.* And where that *Y* joined was the best spot on this part of the river. Down below the water got quite deep again and slow moving. In any of these three places fish would take. But normally if they took in one place, you would not find them in another. You would never be certain where they were lying, and try to switch fly patterns accordingly.

At the end of the day I was more than a little perturbed. "We each got a fish. Let's go."

"I'll try it again," David said, fishing now through the middle stretch of the pool for about the fifteenth time.

I don't know what I bet him, but it was something—that he would not get another fish. I prayed that he would not get another fish. I put a hex on the water and on all his flies.

"No, I'll get another fish," he said calmly.

The morning crowd had left, the afternoon crowd had left, and the evening crowd was getting pretty tired. Still Savage fished through the long pool, cast after cast without comment, came out, sat down, spat his plug, and looked through his fly box again.

There had not been a fish taken since an hour after I had taken my grilse at the top of the pool earlier that day. I looked at my pocket watch, then I would sigh. I would sigh just so Savage would know I was sighing and looking at my pocket watch, perturbed.

But again he would look through his fly box, scratch his head, and put on another fly.

Finally he took out a small bug, about a number 8 or 10, half-brown and half-green, with a bare body.

"I'm going to give this a try," he said, smiling. "Just one more try."

"That's about the worst godforsaken fly I've ever seen," I said.

And out he went into the pool again. Then he got down to his last few casts.

"Come on," I said.

"I'll cast twice more," he said. He threw his line out, the fly gracefully touched the water and moved across the pool in the twilight. The sun was almost gone, the sky red and white, and nighthawks and swallows skimmed the surface of the water, while the trees in the background were solid and dark. He stripped in his line and brought it back.

"Last cast, Mr. Savage," I said.

His fly hit the water. The tip of his rod began to bend and butt. The fish took a run, jumped high in the night air. He turned and smiled, a chew of Red Man plug in his cheek.

Now and then, when I was fishing, I would hit some trout. And on certain lone summer nights I go fishing them myself. The flies we are using for trout are tiny, number 12s or 14s on those occasions. They are called, aptly enough, mosquitoes, mayflies, etc. Some tied are a variation of small flies and have no proper name. Nymphs—you can hardly see them in the water, but in a black pool near an old wood bank on the Bartibog or Bay du Vin these little flies cause the trout to stick their mouths out of the water and suck them in. You fish early or late because of this. A trout is finicky about dinner. Ravenous, yes—finicky as well. But at a point in the evening with that tiny little fly skirting above them, they will suck them down the same way we might accidentally suck a mosquito down. We are looking for three- or four-pound trout.

I like fishing for trout because even more than salmon it provides me with a link to my youth—to my father and brothers, my aunt who fished for trout instead of salmon, because fishing salmon was not considered ladylike when she was a girl. A link to that little eight-inch trout I caught at Beaverbrook Stream when I was four. It is perhaps the most pristine of fishing, the most poetic. You are able to think of fishing stories from the *Saturday Evening Post,* of Norman Rockwell, of long dusty roads, and cool streams, and children. You are able to reflect upon all of this as an essential part of rural life, like sleigh bells and Christmas, or your favourite writers like the catfish-seeking Mark Twain, or the brilliant rural observer, Ernest Buckler. And if that is all sentimental and nostalgic, so be it. Trout fishing can do this for you just at twilight with a tiny nymph fly, a smell of fly dope, and an old warm fishing basket strung over your shoulder.

I will trout fish with my son in the small ponds that lay in woods near the Norwest, with a small yellow-and-red bobbin. I will fish with him along the Kingston Peninsula and in small streams through cow pastures downriver. All of this brings me back to my own childhood. Though I rarely keep a trout any more unless it is near the size of those three- and four-pound trout I caught one June night at B&L. Along the Padapedia last summer I released all but two trout on the three-day canoe trip. That is, I released fourteen trout. Many of them were the size of trout I wouldn't think of throwing back a few years before. But now I am careful. I hold them under the water and remove the fly as tenderly as possible, and hope to myself when I release them from my hand that they will spend a year or two to grow large and strong. I also released a seventeen-pound salmon on that trip and felt not a bit the less for it.

There are big trout in the Bay du Vin, big brown trout. And sometimes we ran it with a flat-bottom boat, early in the spring when the water was high.

The last time I ran this stretch with an acquaintance, years ago now, we pulled in halfway along and made supper. It was a warm evening, every now and then gusts of hot air hitting your face when the breeze picked up. The river was still high enough—just—to run the boat, although a canoe would have been much better.

After supper, just before dark, we got some trout—the largest almost three pounds, taken by my friend before we settled down for the night, in a large hole near the bank. I got a good-sized trout about a pound lighter just above our camp.

I walked up and threw a tiny little butterfly over some rapids we had poled through earlier, and I could see the back of the trout as it came up almost to the top of the water trailing my fly, somewhat like those file films on sharks trailing a piece of meat. My friend was using spinner and worm.

The Bay du Vin River—its lush undergrowth on either side and the orange reddishness of the water, *vin*-coloured—makes one think they are far to the south, on a river in Central America at times. The bugs and mosquitoes might make you think this as well.

We soaked the trout in butter and flour and ate them resting near the water's edge—for near our camp, and everywhere else, the bugs were voracious. Yet we went to bed that night in the open air, and I lay awake listening to the water.

Just before I drifted off to sleep I could hear a movement far away on the hills to my right. It got closer over time, and then closer still. I realized I was listening to a moose making its way down to the river. The flies were bad, and it was probably being driven crazy. It kept getting closer, and still I tried to go to sleep, until it crashed right on top of me—no more than a yard away.

And it wasn't about to stop.

I jumped up and threw a hand out at it. In the darkness I could see its nose about a foot from mine. The young cow put on the brakes and turned and ran.

The next morning I could see where its tracks stopped, digging into the dirt about three feet from my sleeping bag. I guess I had startled it as much as it did me.

Ten

MY FISHING WORLD IS filled with eccentrics and I suppose I am as eccentric as most. But, at this point a more sinister reflection. A reflection about the great woods, and the deep unending trials in these woods. Of animals and man.

One summer—my seventh or eighth fishing—when the weather was rough most of the summer and fishing not very good, I had a visit from Henry. He came to my camp after eight at night. This was the first camp my brothers and I had managed to build near Mullin Stream. It was a small camp with one room, the inside walls made of pressed boards, the table a cut of rough plywood, the cupboards made of two-by-sixes. The ceiling was a run for mice, and we had one propane lantern. Our door, too, like old Mr. Simms's, was always open.

Henry came in and sat with me in the half dark of this camp, in the middle of nowhere, listening to the brook run below us, like a meandering lullaby. Outside dark spruce hugged the yard in a melancholy way, and night was coming on.

He sat there sipping from a bottle of wine and looking about, as if ready to make comment about what our camp lacked or needed in the way of improvement. He was almost bald. His eyes were bright and black. If I ever want to describe something about the world, I know I would have to mention Henry. Henry was a poacher.

He took fish on a pitchfork or in nets that he lay out in a pool, where the salmon had no hope of escaping. The splashing in the water was something similar to dolphins being caught up in a tuna net. He'd down a moose on the side of a dirt road just on a whim, and then take an axe to its head.

He worked at night, the pretence being that he kept it all hidden from someone like me who *disapproved.*

I wrote something about him in *Lives of Short Duration,* or people like Henry. Poachers often are self-justified, and always seem morally affronted when you challenge them. They also wish to make you feel like a prude if you say anything. It is extremely complex and psychological warfare. Also some of the wardens were once poachers themselves, a few years before they became wardens.

He'd asked me if I'd seen such and such or who's and who. He was mentioning wardens by name. When he asked he would cast his eyes here and there as I spoke.

"NO, I haven't seen him."

He would look at the stove.

Or I might say, "Saw the truck yesterday."

He would glance at the door.

I was worried for a variety of reasons. When he was in the woods with me, I knew that if given half a chance, he would try to net a pool. To him, it didn't seem like a challenge unless he was breaking the law. For him, the idea of fishing was not so much to use skill and dexterity to catch fish but to use this skill to violate all the regulations applied to fishing in one day. That dexterity was required only to confront and affront the principles that men invoked to protect themselves from each other, just to test your own will.

Once when we were fishing on a small pool that was open on the Norwest, he left me where I was. After a time calling to him, and getting no answer, only the sad waving of the trees, and the smell of earth just at twilight, I crossed the slippery river and began my trek. And a half-hour later I found Harry looking at a pool.

"This is Crown reserve," I said.

"I know, boy, I know. It's a goddamn shame," he said.

And he began to cast through it. And then looking at me he took out a jig hook—three-pronged, which looked like an anchor—and threw it in, gave a riff, and away went the salmon, jigged in the tail.

Just then a group of American men came down to the pool for an evening fish, and their guide with them.

"Get the hell out of there, Henry," I said.

"I would, I would, by God, I would—but I'm pretty well committed now," he said. The salmon tore the jig hook away after a minute or so. But it was a disturbing minute. After that I tried not to fish with him.

But I must say something else. I liked him—he was very likeable. He had a variety of likeableness about him that would endear anyone to him. He was more than likeable—he was hill-billiable. He dropped twenty dollars into the Salvation Army bowl without a thought, kept care of his brother's family without a thought—was always worried if they had enough clothes or scribblers for school, or if they would have a good Christmas.

Except—for there is always an except here—he was a dyed-in-the-wool poacher.

Once hunting in deer season he shot two moose, and once in moose season he shot two deer.

"I must have got it all mixed up," he said. I suppose he was self-will run riot, but I could not help but like him.

There is a problem about this. He was always on guard and always on watch. By the end of it all he trusted no one, and fought with those he poached with. It seemed a hard price to pay for a fish.

If anyone has ever seen a movie about moonshine runners worried about G-men, then Henry fit the description of a suspicious moonshine runner. He would hide his Jeep, but never hid it well enough. He would circle back to his house, to throw his scent. No matter how often he tried to hide his nets he was always cornered with nets on him. He lived hiding, and staring out of shed windows at dusk, looking for the wardens. In his suspiciousness he had made me realize that some part of him felt guilty about it—that his guilt went beyond the law and into his conscience. And that's when a poacher such as Henry will turn on you—when you see that guilt.

The idea that a poacher has guilt that goes beyond the arm of the law, and into a Dostoyevskian idea of *Crime and Punishment,* fits like a glove on most of their hands after a certain amount of time. That is not to say that a man or a woman can't take an extra fish now and then without suffering the pangs of misery and guilt. If the world wasn't big enough for that, it would be small indeed. But at a certain point, within the dominion of taking *far too much,* poachers like Henry begin to get agitated, feel sick, and the only cure for them is to not poach any more. Like criminals, they must get away as quickly as possible from what it is they have done.

He came to my camp that cool and rainy night, the eighth year of my fishing. He kept staring at the door, asking me questions, and relating that he was listening to me with a slight glance my way. Finally the door opened and a fellow, who looked deranged, came in. He looked at Henry and smiled, glanced at me and frowned.

He had no teeth, his body one giant tattoo.

He reminded me of the escaped prisoner I had once picked up hitchhiking outside of Dorchester (I had no idea he was an escaped prisoner). I asked him where he was going and he said, "Arizona."

I knew just by the way Henry walked he had jig hooks on him, and a net hidden nearby. It was as if I took an X-ray of Henry, I would see all of Henry's bones—his thin rib cage, his legs, his pointy knees, his very bony feet walking back and forth in front of me—and while he was talking about heating up some soup, I would see jig hooks stuck everywhere.

It was the idea of nondisclosure that bothered me as much as anything else. Henry couldn't risk trusting me, and therefore I could not trust him. So then why was he at my camp? Even a poor camp such as it was. A poacher's life is full of contradictions and abnormalities. Nothing is ever exactly right with them. He not only had his wife in on the act, but his children, two skinny little girls, who also seemed to be weighed down with jig hooks—and in hunting season, leaves of lettuce and cabbage sticking in their braids and apple cores from between their ears.

In effect, Henry had managed to make his whole family lawless by his self-will. And I often felt that all of them were in hiding more than most of us, most of their lives. It made me realize that freedom, as he believed it to be, was an awful cross to bear and came at a tremendous price.

Henry's *friend* began jumping up and down on the cot: "Gonna get a fish."

"That's nice," I would say.

"Settle down now, Melvin," Henry would say, looking over at me suspiciously.

"Gonna get a fish."

I wanted to tell Henry that this man was insane. An absolute nut bar. And it was a small camp. But then I considered, Henry wasn't entirely sane himself.

Melvin went outside at midnight—all was quiet for a moment.

"Where the hell is he going?"

"Who?"

"Your fellow traveller," I said.

"You like him?" Henry said expectantly.

"What's not to like?"

"Probably going for a leak."

I nodded and said nothing more.

And then *bang bang bang kerpow kerpow*. Five rifle shots rang out.

"What the hell was that?"

"The rifle." Henry yawned.

"Has he brought a rifle?"

"Of course." Yawn.

"I see"—yawn—"Why?"

"Wants to target practice, likes to keep his hand in. I thought I might allow him, you know, to shoot one."

"Sure." Yawn, yawn. "Shoot one what?"

"Shoot a salmon. Just don't look at him when he comes in. Don't look and he won't bother you. *I* can't do a thing with him."

"Why not?"

"Well, he's manslaughtered before. But if I say anything, Mommie always gets all upset."

"Mommie—who's Mommie?"

"Our mommie—Mommie Fallon. He's my brother."

The night was turning sour. You lie down with dogs as they say.

It was raining very hard outside, and we were supposed to go to the south branch of the Sevogle the next morning. The water would be high and roaring and cloudy, the worst kind of day for fishing. The pans were all on the floor because of the seventeen drips in my roof, and I lay in my bunk, wondering aloud why I had ever stopped drinking.

I didn't want Mommie Fallon to be upset. But the man couldn't stay in our camp with his salmon-shooting rifle. But God was with me.

Suddenly Melvin said, "I think I overdosed."

"Oh—on what?" I queried.

"Many, many mushrooms."

"What kind of many, many mushrooms?"

"Many magic mushrooms. I gotta go."

"Go where?"

"I gotta go home—right now."

And he jumped up, fell into the stove, then bolted out the door into the dark.

"Those damnable magic mushrooms," Henry said, and got up and put on his boots.

And we went out to find Melvin cowering behind the truck.

On the way home Melvin sat in the back, Henry on the passenger side, and I drove. But that wasn't the worst of it. The worst of it was when Melvin found my bucksaw. He no longer liked the woods—wanted to get out of them as quickly as possible. Now he started something that was slightly comic, and more than a little disturbing.

My new friend Melvin kept trying to saw through his brother's head. Not his entire head, but just increment by increment, with the bucksaw.

"I hate it here—it's all closing in on me—get me out of here—don't look at me—don't you *look* at me."

"Stop sawing my head off, Melvin."

"Don't you look at me."

"Stop sawing my head."

As soon as we got to Castle Street he fled into the night. I never saw him again.

"You just haven't seen him at his very best," Henry said.

It was pouring rain by this time, and I never got fishing the next day, or the next. Then one day I went up and walked from Milk Jug down to Three Minute Pool, and back up. I hooked a grilse on the way back. Then it tore about, running with my line until I lost it. I never went back to the South Branch until some years later my dog Jeb Stuart and I saw a bear cub walking down to Teacup Pool.

Henry was caught later that year bringing three salmon out in the back of his car. He said he didn't know how they got there and pleaded not guilty, even though he had a net wrapped up in a sleeping bag.

"What did you think when you saw the fish there?" his lawyer asked.

"It absolutely bowled me over—not once but a number of times," Henry said. "I couldn't believe it at all."

"And you didn't try to bite the warden?"

"Bite a warden—why would I want to bite a warden? You bite a warden, you're biting off more than you can chew."

I don't know how to *explain* Henry other than the way I have. Just as I might wish there be a pill to cure him, I wish there might be a pill to explain him. One of the only other ways I can explain him is in his trying to justify what he was doing. One night after he and a friend of his had taken salmon, and then fought over them, Henry began to talk about his friend being greedy, unlike he was—that *he himself* was not greedy—and there was a great difference between *why* he wanted to poach and the poaching of his friend. After a while he became more and more upset and morally outraged. And I think that his dilemma, and dementia, is part of the larger dilemma of self-justification at the expense of others.

It is very hard to look at greed in the face of a poacher or anyone else.

In these woods I have met men who never care to speak, and men who just cannot shut up, men who dress like eighteenth-century farmers in old straw hats, and men who have the most high-tech equipment possible. All of them are seen on the river, following their own dreams, looking for the fabled fish that they dreamed about since they thought and spoke as a child.

I know a great guide who cannot stand to get into a canoe because he's never learned to pole, and another who, on more than one occasion, parked his canoe halfway down the Norwest River and slept in it all night with his sport, so his sport could fish a pool at dawn. And all of them have one thing in common, and that one thing is the salmon. It is the great salmon that brings them together, that is inclusive in a way few other things in life are. No man or woman here minds if you haven't read Henry James. And most don't even mind if you have.

Eleven

ONCE WHEN I WAS fishing with my dog—the toughest little dog I ever had, a little river-water dog named after the rebel calvary officer Jeb Stuart—we met a bear and a cub on those hills above the South Branch. Unlike Peter's bear, it was still very much alive.

Jeb was a good dog to have with me. And since I do much of my fishing alone now, I like having a dog. Old Jeb is gone now, and I have another dog with me, Roo, who is a great companion—she has also gotten me back to my truck quicker than I would have made it when fishing the Sevogle.

Some years back, when friends of ours were visiting at our cottage on the bay, I decided to get them a fish to barbecue. I left early in the morning with Jeb beside me, and travelled to the Norwest. All the morning I fished hard and saw nothing, and so disheartened I went back to the cottage in late afternoon with nothing to show.

"I will try it again tomorrow," I said. "I will switch rivers—go to the Little Souwest."

And so I did. The next day I fished three pools on the Little Souwest. But still there was no luck for me.

So home I went. My friends looked at me a little sheepishly and began to say they didn't want any fish anyway. But that did nothing more than get my blood up.

"I'll get a fish tomorrow," I said, "even if I have to crawl to the river and back."

Such was my statement—now to do it.

I left very early in the morning for the long drive to the Sevogle. This was in July; this is where the fish were. I was just being lazy not going there in the first place.

At that time I had not been at the Sevogle in a few years, and the road—the logging road Peter had found that night years before—was overgrown and swamped.

My old truck went into four-wheel drive, but even so, it was a hard road. My little dog Jeb bounced up and down on the seat as I bounced along, the two mirrors flattened right out to the side of my windows, and I could smell the engine working overtime as the bush got thicker and thicker.

By the time I reached the path down to Milk Jug Pool I could go no further; I had wanted to travel into White Birch, but it seemed to me that there was no road left—not the road I once knew. And so I thought that Milk Jug Pool is a good pool too, and so is Teacup, and I've taken fish from them as well.

Jeb and I got out. I was a little excited because I knew we'd see fish here. I put on my vest, checked my lunch, Jeb's dog biscuits, and my box of flies, told my dog to go ahead and down over the hill we went. On one corner going towards the river on that steep path there is a crooked tree people lean against where they can first see and hear the river, which looks to be about three stories beneath them. The rapids flow over brown rocks at the top of the pool, where you cross to fish down through from the far side, and there is no better sound in the world to a fisherman who is just coming on it.

The birds were singing and it was early morning when I made my way, with Jeb swimming beside me, across to the far side of that pool, got my fly box out, looked through it for a fly, and suddenly realized that I had forgotten my rod at the truck.

Of course I am an idiot—but I cannot tell you how being an idiot makes you feel.

"Dammit, Jeb," I said. I could not believe that I had forgotten my rod leaning against the side of the truck, or that I was so excited to get to the pool I had not missed it anywhere on the steep climb down.

"Come on, Jeb," I said, and back up we started. It was a long climb back and when we got to the top, my rod leaned against the front of the truck as if it was making fun of human effort.

Actually I was so angry I didn't want to go back down.

"If I have to crawl to the river and back," I remembered my Hannibalistic-sized boast the night before.

The sun was now high and it was warm.

"Come on, boy," I said, and down Jeb Stuart and I went. The foliage was thick and green, the water inviting, when all of a sudden Jeb, who usually stuck close to me, veered off to the right and a small black animal started off in front of him. I thought it was a porcupine and wondered if I had any pliers with me to dig out the quills, or whether or not Jeb who was a tough mutt of a dog would allow me to touch his snout if that happened, when I heard the animal give a squeal and realized it was a bear cub.

"Jeb," I said, in a short low voice, "you get over here." Jeb paid me no mind at all. And then I heard the mother. I was not in a great position. Jeb barked and barked, and then a minute later back he came, running. My major concern was that he would bring the angry female right to me. I heard the cracking of trees a short distance away. Jeb ran behind me, growling and wagging his tail.

"Let's go," I said. And down we went. When we got to that tree, I heard the bear and its cub crossing the path above us. They moved away, and down we went to the pool. When we got to the other side I stared back and could hear them again, and for at least five more minutes as the female, far above us, crossed the path once more and back to where it had come from. After a while the sound of them became faint, and then indistinguishable, with the slight waving of the trees.

The pool is small, and doesn't look like all that much, but in the middle and along the far side there is a fine run of water and fish lay there. The water was brown-toned in the sunlight, and kept gurgling songs at me, as I waded into the rapids at the top of the pool.

I cast three or four times, with a number 8 bug with an orange hackle and white body, and suddenly, eureka, the line tightened, and I had on a grilse that I had no trouble landing. I often play my fish hard, grilse especially, and land them as soon as their nose is turned towards me.

I killed the grilse and made a bed, rested the pool, and had a cup of coffee and a chew of plug and fished down through the pool again. The trees were in great midsummer form, the water ripe for fishing, and there wasn't a sound of a human being.

Twelve

THE NEXT SEASON I had a canoe, and went to the Norwest early, to go down and get fiddleheads in the soil above Wilson's Pool. I was going to take some of these fiddleheads to Mr. Simms, and I remembered the story Premier Richard Hatfield once told me about fiddleheads—that the Micmac Indian believed the fiddlehead, and the way the top of the stem curled inward on itself, was a map of how moose travelled in the woods. It seemed a wonderful explanation to me, about how the gods linked moose and fiddlehead and river and province together.

The water that day was high, so the river was no trouble running, and it was swift and fun. I had a rod with me, but had little luck, so I picked a garbage bag of fiddleheads, and spent the day on the river alone, with homemade jam and bread and scalding coffee, feeling very comfortable and free (as Huck would say).

A man came along in an old-town canoe with his wife and little girl, winging through the fast water that flowed seemlessly near the gunnels. All around me were signs of the new world. Maples were leafing in the distance, and poplars. The air ticked with bugs, but the blackflies weren't out yet to drive you crazy.

Further along a moose crossed the river in front of my canoe without even caring to notice me—except for a side glance. And further along still an osprey circled in the warm sun above its nest while here and there among the shadows small patches of resilient snow stubbornly hugged the rocks.

So I was free, I guess. That's what we all want. And lucky too. For so much of our dealings with wilderness is taken up in trying to find it. Humankind has stretched itself to the ends of it all. David Carroll in his wonderfully poetic book on trout fishing talks about how pure the world was when the natives were here alone, and how the Europeans scorched the earth barren, so that you have to navigate dams and go fishing with houses next to you and the smell of factories, mills, and gas. The Miramichi has not escaped this either.

Another observation Mr. Carroll makes that I cannot help but agree with is that lake fishing did not move him, like stream fishing. It was too vast and dark for him to get a feeling for. I have lake fished enough to know what he is saying. There is something about the movement of the water, pertaining to the movement and spawn of fish, that is missing in lake fish.

I met up with the canoe with the young family. They were hauled up on a small rocky beach just above Dennis Pool, and were free of the world, and all the troubles of the world, by being immersed in the natural one.

The little girl sat on a rock as the mother took out the Coleman stove and got it going. The man got his rod out and, putting on a Mickey Finn streamer, waded out and cast into the heavy water, and was soon around a bend hidden by some trees only to reappear a little later, walking through the snow-spotted and puddle-laden woods.

I pulled in along side them and we spoke for a while, while I had a chew of Red Man plug. The sun made shadows on the little girl's clothing as she sat with a cup of hot chocolate, and there wasn't another voice or sound for miles, except that of the river.

I made it down to Wayerton Bridge sooner than I thought

I would and waited for my brother to come along and drive me back around to my truck.

Then I went home and took some of the fiddleheads over to Mr. Simms, who was sitting inside the porch with a blanket over him. I thought of the little girl sitting on the beach above Dennis Pool and how many times Mr. Simms had poled down past it. How strong he was as a river guide, and how he would have managed to take care of parties of four or five fishermen or hunters all of his life.

But now he was suffering from Alzheimer's, and it is a terrible illness.

His brother had noticed that there was something wrong first. When Mr. Simms retired all he spoke about was going into the woods in the spring, and spending his days on the river. But then he had found out he didn't have riparian rights. And he had travelled with me to the South Branch and seen how much of it was clear-cut, which he said would destroy fishing for good. And then, the worst thing happened. That fall, when he was hunting, he lost his commemorative tin cup.

So he wouldn't go to his camp. And his brother kept wondering why. His brother would come to visit him, and say, "Come on, let's go." And Mr. Simms would always make an excuse. The water was probably too high, or they hadn't had rain, or there was too much work to do about the house.

The next fall he asked his brother to build him a tree stand for deer hunting, and when his brother asked where he wanted it, Mr. Simms pointed to a tree fifteen yards from their camp.

Then his brother knew that there was something terrible the matter and Mr. Simms was frightened of getting lost. Soon Mr. Simms gave up going to the woods, gave up driving, and did nothing but walk up and down the lane, while his brother had to take care to see he didn't wander too far and get lost.

I gave Mr. Simms the fiddleheads, and spoke to him about fishing, but now I could tell it was an act with him more than anything else. And he was going over an old ritual with me that he would forget, and that all the dreams of the river, and his fifty years on it, were gone. They had drifted away to others, like myself, and he was alone.

I left him with some chewing tobacco—and I don't believe I saw him again.

I was addicted to Red Man plug, Copenhagen snuff, cigars, and cigarettes. I believed I couldn't catch a fish without a chew of plug in. I would quit during the winter, but the first moment I saw the river begin to open I would look at my rod, reels, flies, and vest, check my waders for holes, and go out and buy some Red Man loose-leaf or plug. Then I would spit for five months.

If I was called away to a meeting in Toronto, I was in a terrible state. I would sit in an office, and mumble, "'Scuse me—I got to spit."

I was never comfortable without it, and certainly not comfortable with it between my jaws in an office on the ninth floor of a publishing house. I made serious heroic attempts to quit each summer, and every time I did my mind wandered, and my fishing got lousy.

But all superstitions are validated by the superstitious. I believed I could not get a fish without a chew of plug. This started my first year fishing, and has remained with me ever since. And since I have a problem with tobacco—I started to smoke when I was three—I have a hard time letting go.

A man will wear a certain hat, another a certain kind of boot. Others will make sure they go to Mass before they go fishing or as soon as they get home.

Over time it becomes as essential to them as the water they intend to fish. Or they will take one path through the woods to a pool instead of another:

"If I go down that path I won't get fish," they will rationalize, because of some remote occurrence in their past, and it all seems logical and highly probable to them. I know a dozen fishermen like this.

Peter used to make sacrifices to the water. Perhaps he still does. Only little ones. Not a goat or a herd of sheep. But a pack of cigarettes. And he would shake his head at me if I didn't. To him I was blasphemous.

People, myself included, have to have certain things on them to feel that they will have luck. An old fly they never used any longer, or a certain buck knife. For me it was a pair of clippers I wore around my neck on a brown shoestring.

One night, the previous season, I had fished Doug Underhill's camp pool on the Renous with an older man named Simon, coming out on the other side of the river to fish his productive run below Simon's rock. There were other people on the river as well. Jim McQuaid who owns the camp with Doug and others had taken fish. At the lower part of the run, gone orange in the late sunlight, I had a hit. I fished over this fish for a while, and looking back saw that Underhill had hooked a grilse halfway down the pool. I stepped down, and reeled in my line. A man at the camp above came down to ask if he might borrow my clippers.

I handed them over and forgot to get them back.

The next spring as I was checking things over I couldn't find them. I had had them for eleven years. I went from place to place in the house, feeling generally miserable.

"What's wrong?" my wife asked.

"I can't find my fingernail clippers," I said.

"Well, why don't you just take a pair of mine?"

But I could never get comfortable with a new pair.

A few weeks after I ran the river to get fiddleheads, my brother John decided to run the river with me.

We took my canoe and put in at Miner's Bridge. It was a warm day in late June. And lots of people were running the river. So all of the pools would be well fished or paddled through by the time we got to them.

I had a pair of my wife's fingernail clippers in my vest and away we went.

I fished Ledge Pool and then the little run where I hooked a grilse beside the rock that first year, the one that made a leap and split my fly.

When we got to Dr. Wilson's I was being bitten very badly by flies. The sun was warm, and I took off my waders and went into the water in jeans. The water wasn't that cool. And besides, I feel that once your legs go numb you're halfway home.

I began to fish down through the pool. There is a small rock just out from shore once you get past the deeper boulders in the middle of the pool, where I have hooked half a dozen fish. But by the time I got down to it, I felt out of sorts.

I came into shore and asked John for some fly dope. I was bitten on the face and neck and hands.

"You've got to eat," John said.

I took the Deep Woods Off and poured it over my wounds, got into the bow of the canoe, and away we went. The day was clear and warm and the water was the right level to run a canoe fairly easily.

I shook my head, had a drink of coffee, but I felt miserable when we came to Stickney Pool.

The water was high enough that I couldn't see one of the boulders just jutting above the water when we came into the pool. The canoe ground on it, and John jabbed his paddle down and backed the canoe up before it turned sideways in the rapid.

"David, you should have seen that," John said.

I didn't reply because I felt my throat was swelling up.

"Aren't you going to fish here?" he said.

"Let's just keep going."

Nor did I fish the long productive stretch below it.

So we reached Cedar Pool a little while later.

John and I came in on the beach, and watched a few canoes pass down ahead of us. Now I felt very warm and took off my shirt.

I walked back and forth on the beach trying to get some

air and a man came in from the pool and looked at me.

"What happened to you?"

My body was covered in red welts and my legs were starting to give.

"Let's go," John said.

When we got to the nice little run below Cedar there was a rock in the centre of the river. I paddled the canoe right into it without seeing it. I couldn't see anything at the moment. Three men we knew were fishing that run and they were a little upset, to say the least. I never cared for them very much anyway, and John had had a run in with one before, so it wasn't much to start an argument.

"Learn how to run a canoe," one of them said. "I thought I was bad."

John jumped to my defence.

"You are bad," he said, standing in the canoe. "You are about as bad as they come. Come over here and I'll show you how bad you are!"

And then he got out and pulled the canoe away. Now I couldn't see and couldn't breathe. My right hand was swelled like a pumpkin, and I kept splashing water on my face.

"The bugs finally got ya," John said.

Well, the bugs finally did get me or as I now suspect the deet in the fly dope. I could only breathe every little while, with my throat swelling. I put the paddle away and let John handle the canoe from then on.

When we got to Peter's camp an hour later, he was fishing his pool, and actually had a salmon on.

"You look like death warmed over," he said when he saw me. I told him I was bitten by a bug.

"A bug," he said. "Not a bear, a moose, a mouse—not even a turtle—a bug."

I reminded him succinctly that Alexander the Great died of a mosquito bite, so it must be an honourable demise.

We got to his truck and headed to the hospital, with my head out the window trying to get air. Peter was glancing over at me and thinking up a storm.

"What we'll have to get you—I guess—is a giant bubble," Peter said. "You can bubble yourself up, and bob downriver. You'll be the bubble boy of the Miramichi. I can make you a bubble at work if you want. It's no problem. We'll have those accordion-like arms, with giant rubber gloves, so you can cast, and I'll put duck feet on the bottom so you can walk."

When I got to the hospital the doctor cavalierly said, "Oh you just had a reaction. People usually live through the first one, but I'm going to give you a prescription for an adrenaline needle. Keep it on you in the woods, because the next reaction might be deadly."

I have taken the needle into the woods with me. But I still don't use fly dope. And though a nurse said to me, "You just never know what they're putting in a bug nowadays," I still have a feeling it was the deet.

I couldn't get going that summer, though I spent more time on the water with the canoe than I ever did before. That reaction seemed to sap strength from me and often I was exhausted when I got to the river.

One day that summer Peter watched me fish down through Black's Pool. I thought I had covered the water okay, and my line seemed to be working well. I worked my way down carefully, certain I had covered the stretch. But when I came in, Peter said, "Give me your rod a second—"

He walked above me and crossed the river, with his head down, as it usually was, looking into the water. Then he took my rod, waved the bug back and forth above his head to dry it out, and cast into a small run I had missed.

As soon as his fly touched I knew he was going to hook a salmon, and he did.

In the end it was all because I had lost my nail clippers with the brown shoestring.

When Peggy came up to join me on the river one day, Peter took pity upon me and gave me one of his fish.

"Here—never mind. Barbecue this for Peg," he said.

A friend of his teased me, saying, "God, have you stooped to this degree? Do you have to get Peter to get yer fish for Peg?"

That was enough.

"I'll pay you back tomorrow," I said as I left the camp.

I went home and barbecued the fish for Peggy and her mother, set the clock for five in the morning. Then I got up and took Roo in the truck with me and headed for the Norwest. I had the key for Stickney road, and drove into Wilson's Pool. Then Roo and I walked down to Stickney.

We walked down to the run above Cedar, and I fished Cedar Pool.

Then we walked back to the truck and had lunch. The day was warm and cloudless. I watched the pool above as I ate. This was the first year in ten years I had not taken a fish from Wilson's Pool. I knew my fly crossed the nose of many fish that day alone. But I was, in the parlance of Hemingway, the worst kind of unlucky.

I drove around to the run above Hawthorn's. After I fished there I went to Black's large pool. I fished Black's for an hour. It is a great pool to fish, but I often found it was deceptively *too* good. That is, more people seem to fish it than get fish from it. Perhaps it is because you are uncertain where fish are because you can look upon it as being a pool in three sections.

I left and drove all the way around again, and fished the Turnip Patch Pool, especially the lower end where fish had been taken earlier. Turnip Patch always seemed an unpleasant stretch to fish, though it is productive. You hug close to the right bank coming down, and have to be aware of your back cast, unless you're left handed. Your line moves too fast in the rough water and your fly can get dragged behind it. But the lower part is fine, and you can work your line better.

Then I went into the Miner's camp pool. That was the day Roo wouldn't allow the Americans, who had come to fish from Maine, to come near it. She was trying to protect me, I think. I put Roo in the truck, put in some plug, and went down it twice.

Then I went to Allison's and fished. A herd of people were there. They had been chasing the fish back down with their boots. The theory being that fish would get so frustrated that they'd finally take.

I then thought of Caul's Pool above the Miner's Bridge. So away I went.

Roo and I walked into Caul's. It was almost deserted. An Indian man was fly-fishing there alone.

"Anything?" I asked.

"A few were taken this morning, but it's pretty slow," he said.

But I gave it a try. Then we left.

"Where else can we go, Roo?" I said.

Roo didn't comment but just stared out the window, ignoring me. She was mad because I'd put her in the truck. So I gave her part of my last bologna sandwich, and poured a little Pepsi in my hat for her to slurp.

"Have a slurp of Pepsi, Roo," I said. "Lick about the fly dope."

There was only one place left. I went, tail between Roo's legs, to Peter's camp pool at eight that evening.

Peter was finishing supper dishes. His camp is so spotless it looks like a museum. The great moose rack that I took from the thousand-pound bull is there, along with stuffed birds, pictures of salmon and deer. It is such an immaculate camp that you could eat off the floor; if a blind is a quarter of a centimetre from being perfectly straight, Peter will work an hour to get it just so. He owns his camp with Les Druet who is even a better woodsman than he is.

"Are you going down to the pool?" I asked.

"Most definitely," he said.

And we started out with Roo and George trailing behind

us. Peter took the lower part of the pool and I went to the very top, about two hundred yards from him. I took off my bug and put on a small Green Butt Butterfly, with white wings that seemed as soft as fairy dust.

Roo and George were behind us running about in the woods. And I started along. The water at the upper end of the pool is flat and flows deep below Portage River, and now looked dark and full, because night was coming on. There is a rock in the middle of this run, and a set of smaller rocks further out and down. It is a meandering part of the river, butterfly country—no doubt about it.

I was throwing my line towards the far rocks, and letting the fly move along in the slow darkening current. Far above me an osprey circled, and above the pool a poor little doe gone crazy with night flies swam across the river into the woods, and came out ten minutes later below Peter and swam across the river again.

"Poor damn thing," Peter yelled out to me. I nodded and cast again, let my fly cover the water, stripped my line and began to bring it back, when I felt a hard pull.

"That's a trout," Peter, who was still turned towards me, said.

"No—it didn't take like a trout—it's a grilse," I said.

"It's not acting like a grilse."

"That's because its swimming right towards me," I said.

I reeled in as much line as I could before the grilse started to jump. Then Peter walked up the shore, and I made my way to the beach.

I brought the fish in, killed it, tagged it, before Peter got to me. The day was growing dark. The osprey had gone home.

"Here you go," I said, handing the fish to him, looking at the red sky with the sun gone down.

I'd had about ten minutes to spare.

The next afternoon, Doug Underhill phoned to say he had found my clippers.

Thirteen

THERE WAS ONE MORE time I used a spin cast. It was that year and Peg and I were staying at her mom's, close by the Bartibog River. The trout were coming in, and I wanted to try my hand. But I wanted Peg to fish with me.

She had run the Bartibog River in the canoe the previous summer with me, and I decided that I would encourage this.

"Let's get out tomorrow," I said. "We'll take the rowboat and just go above the bridge. I'll dig some worms and we'll get some trout."

"Sure," Peg said, who was playing crib with her sister and

having a few beer. It seemed like a great idea at that instant.

So I went out in the evening and got some worms, took my spin cast, and searched about for a rod for Peg. Above the rafters in the cellar was an old bamboo rod—not much good for anything, with an old manual reel, and the line all crinkled—that someone put away before they travelled to Ontario to make their fortune.

"That's a good rod for Peg," I said.

Peg was still having some crib and beer when I got it ready, went down to check the oar locks and anchor on the rowboat, looked at the grand and gracious Bartibog.

What a beautiful river, I thought, this little tributary that runs into the main Miramichi just before it widens out into a saltwater bay. I looked out to where we would fish, and decided where I would drop anchor the next morning.

When I went home Peg was still playing cribbage. So I went up to the bedroom and set the clock. Setting a clock for someone else, you become something like—God Almighty. I set it for 5:00, and then thought I would give her a few more minutes sleep, so I set it for 5:15. Then I felt that perhaps I could give her a few more minutes to snooze. So I set it finally for 5:30.

Peg came upstairs about one o'clock, worn out from cribbage, and crawled into bed.

"Fishing tomorrow," I said.

"Herumpph," she answered.

Then I sang that old Bartibog refrain:

In 1814 I took a little trip
Along with Peggy McIntyre on a little fishing trip
We took a little bologna and took a little beans
We had no butter so we took some margarine,
We threw our lines and the fish keep a bitin'
There wasn't as many as there was a while ago
We threw once more and they began a swimmin'
Back the Bartibog to Maggie Aggin's hole,
To Maggie Aggin's hole,
To Maggie Aggin's hole.

Then with my wonderful baritone, I began a beat like the military drum: "*Baroomp boomp bom—baroomp boomp boom.*"

"Herumpph," she answered.

I was up before the alarm went off and got some molasses sandwiches ready, along with a thermos of tea. I got my fishing rod ready and my vest, looked through my wondrous swivels and lures, put my second- or third-best hook and a small sinker on Peg's line, and went to wake her.

The alarm clock was ringing, and her hand was reaching out and her fingers grasping at the air trying to turn it off. She had the covers over her head, but her feet were bare. I sat on the end of the bed and began to tickle them.

"Time to get up and go fishing," I said. "*Baroomp boomp bom—baroomp bomp bom.*"

"Slllleeep," she said.

I gingerly hauled her by the ankles and she plopped on the floor. Then I went downstairs again. When I came up she was curled in a ball beside the bed.

I lifted her by the arms and dragged her into the next bedroom where there was a sink.

"Little water for you," I said, taking one of the sponges and ever so lightly mashing it into her face.

"Ga-gurgle," she said.

"You see how much fun we can have," I said. "Fishing is what *makes* a marriage. Nicki fishes with Peter." I lied. "Ellen fishes with Tony." I lied.

Finally unable to go back to sleep Peggy got dressed, had a bowl of cereal. When she picked up her sixth spoonful of Rice Krispies I couldn't stand the munch sound any more and I took her bowl away.

"That's enough of that," I said.

Out we went towards the Bartibog, me carrying my box of lures and high-tech fishing equipment and Peg dragging her bamboo pole.

"Me using my rod, and you using your pole," I said. "We'll bamboozle them."

For some reason she wasn't speaking to me.

She sat at the back of the little twelve-foot rowboat and out we went to the middle of the river.

My rod ready, I let go an enormous cast and began to reel in slowly, then quickly, while Peg was trying to put a worm on the hook I had provided.

"My hook's all bent up, rusted and crooked," she said.

"Now, now," I cautioned. "Don't start complaining, it's such a wonderful morning."

I was casting away. The water was still, the sun sparkling on it, the trees in the distance lighting up. Peggy dropped her line over the side of the boat. I watched her pathetic worm drop down, turning in circles like a sinking piece of metal, and I sighed.

"Oh—oh—oh," she said, and her rod bowed, and just as quick as that she had a trout about one and a half pounds in the boat.

"Nicely done," I said.

And I cast my line again.

She took the trout off the hook, replaced the worm, and deployed her line in the same place, looking down into the water, with her arms tensed ready to haul another fish up. I smiled.

"I think you'll probably have to cast out further, my dear." And I showed her how well, how expertly I could cast. Then I reeled my line in.

"Oh—oh—oh," Peg said, and she riffed another fish aboard. It was larger than the first one.

"Nice too," I said.

Again she got ready and again she tensed up, her shoulders moving back and forth, ready for the fish to strike.

"Oh—oh—oh," she said. This fish though she couldn't just riff in. It was too big. It ran and jumped and played upon the water, went under the boat, and then finally she hauled it over the side. It weighed about two and a half pounds.

I left the boat later and walked up to the corner to fish in peace. I took my swivel, my eggs, my lures off and put them away. I tried to find the oldest hook I could find.

Then I went back to the boat.

Peg was still hauling in fish. She had a string of about eight or nine. They lay all about her feet, and at various parts of the rowboat.

"How's your luck been?" she asked innocently.

I sat as close to her as I could, and let my line sink as close to her line as possible. So I wouldn't foul her I kept pushing her rod slightly away, towards the back of the boat. But the unfortunate fish didn't know what they were doing. Peg's old rod bent again.

To make matters worse she was munching on a molasses sandwich as she hauled this fish aboard, holding the sandwich in her teeth with her little jar of Red Rose tea beside her.

After a while she said, "David, I'm tired of catching trout."

I insisted in gentlemanly graciousness that I carry the string of eleven trout up the road for her, waving them in the air as I passed people.

Fourteen

FISHING SEASON GAVE way to hunting again that year. Once you could smell the frost in the air, the wind spoiling through the old henhouse and down along the beach where the rocks were cold and the bay was black, it was time to put away the rod and take the rifle out.

I have known great fishermen in my life. Most of them are also hunters. If a man or woman is to eat flesh, he or she is morally obligated at a *certain* time to kill that which they eat. This is what I believe to be true, even though it is perhaps as disgraced an opinion now as any opinion was. However it shouldn't be, for there are still butchers and slaughterhouses aplenty.

Tolstoy, making the same comment in *War and Peace*, spoke about the man or woman who would sentimentally decry hunting while cutting into a steak with gusto.

It is a terrible fact that there is no *thinking* that can't reduce and won't reduce truth, if knowledge is not applied.

I became for a while as passionately an advocate of hunting as I was of fishing. (Or maybe even more so, because it was the more beset upon tradition.) I suppose it is because both rest in my consciousness as being part of the same experience, of town or rural living, that the decision makers in the cities have tried to thwart. Mr. Simms wore a bush jacket and chewed plug. He had never travelled any further than Moncton, and that was when he went to the hospital near the very end of his life. He was as conscious of the world about him as few people are, and was as kind as anyone. Perhaps then my defence is for him.

The urban ideals have crept upon us, much like an army, and instilled our lives with other reflections, from pop culture to McDonald's, so that we have been occupied by the ideas of people who never having lived one day like us, feel nothing in holding us in contempt. The Miramichi and the Ozarks are often compared at a point of smug, vastly ignorant superiority.

So certain people from the Miramichi (and the Ozarks) continually try to prove that they are the same as the urbans. That they too can fly in planes and go to see musicals such as *The Phantom of the Opera.* That they too loathe the rustics.

So too many of the people I know from here, who have joined this common ground, have done so in a way, I suppose, to survive. And the old way—such as it was, of people I admired like Mr. Simms—is disappearing entirely not only from our landscape but our heritage. It is looked upon with embarrassment, made fun of in novels (which pretend to adore it), and is laughed at by the very children of those men.

Of course time itself helps make ghosts of us all.

In defending these disappearing principles, and showing the new ones to be no more worthy of benediction, by rurals who are sometimes ashamed of everything they think has to do with themselves, I have been called a provincial—among those who have adapted themselves to the new world. But I wear this, if I can say, like a badge of honour.

Hunting and fishing were certainly as much a part of the world of my youth as hockey or marbles. And I realize this now more as time goes on—that is, that both have to be defended, not only regulated.

I suppose some will think hunting wrong. But no more so than fishing. And I make the case that until we are all vegetarians by our own choice, both hunting and fishing in some sense are a philosophical duty. At least once in your life.

I do not like how the world views its hunters, and by proxy its fishermen, and I do not like how the hunters and fishermen at times disrespect themselves and what the intended purpose of a hunt is.

But I rarely listen to a fisherman who tells me about how disgusted he is with hunters. Then I say to them, give up your rod and reel, for you are fishing the king of all fish—a fish so majestic it is a wound in the heart at times to see die. Sometimes they will look at me as if I am a raving lunatic, and sometimes they won't. Sometimes, of course, they fish with barbless hooks.

Everything one kills somehow alters that species forever, alters it in the most irreparable way—genetically. But to not kill for most humans is to not live. That's the exceptional dilemma of all people who have entertained both sides.

I often think of this when I think of the desire to fish compared to the actuality of life and death. And often now people let their fish go, or mistake what the purpose of fishing means for the fish.

I would never question anyone about *not* killing something. In this I agree with Laurence Sterne, the eighteenth-century writer who, letting the housefly go, said: "There is room still in the world for me and *you*."

Still we are in a predicament with this, and in a moral quandary always. The dilemma rests upon a point in men's integrity. That which they do has to be acceptable to themselves. That is why it becomes a point for great debate and self-examination. The examination must rest upon the criteria of whether or not this is justified as an act in itself.

Fishing trout years ago with my wife Peggy, on a fertile little brook called McBean, that ran into the Nashwaak River, I was able to pick up some nice trout. The brook was productive, and we camped out in a tent in a field near the stream.

The day we were packing to leave we met a man who had fished behind us that morning, and had taken twenty fish the size of which my wife and I had released. I never forgave him for that because it seemed so bulling and silly. But for himself he felt he had had a grand morning, and was proud of his small shrivelled catch.

Once when I took a fish just at dark, on a small stretch of the Souwest, I killed it, by snapping back its head, and in this way cutting its throat. A person looked at me and said, "Can't you kill it in a more humane way?"

"You can kill it with a rock," I answered. "But this is at least as quick if not quicker—and so, as humane."

I mentioned this the next week when we were fishing trout to another acquaintance. We had taken many nice trout on small white-and-brown number 10 flies all day and were camped on the Bay du Vin in the evening. The smoke from the fire drifted off to our south, the air was still, and the smell of trout frying in butter and flour mingled with the smell of poplars and the long shadows.

"Imagine—feeling sorry for a fish," my acquaintance said abruptly, missing the crux of my argument. This is not what I meant. I certainly have felt sorry for fish.

I have in my lifetime killed enough to have made some observances.

What I am saying is that all of these questions are questions which can only be answered by individual experience and observation, by individuals themselves. It is something that will never be regulated.

I suppose the difference comes not in the act, but in the *reason* for the act. The reason *is* everything. That is why any sport fishing or game hunting is at times so hard to defend.

For instance, I know men who guide other men to bear baits. The men wait in the trees with their camouflaged vests and scarves while their guides wait with them—dressed usually in woollen bush jackets as guides here are. The bear comes into the bait and the sport fires an arrow at the thing's heart. The bear, arrow in it, runs off to claw at it in the bushes. Later when its breathing is rough and uneven, the guide, with his .308, will go in and finish the thing off. That to me, is play-acting of the worst kind.

But in a sense, if you wish to get technical, we all play-act not only in fishing or hunting, but in our entire lives.

I have not bought a poached salmon in my life. Though I know many who do poach them up on the pools at night—some of the very pools I have gone fishing in during the day. I have sat and drank with poachers, and their arguments are often the same. It is their right to do so, because the law favours others—rich sportsmen or native Indians. Also there is the idea that they do not hurt the river more than anyone else. That to me is a particularly self-seeking rationalization. But still, their excuse is not without foundation, that they were the ones left out of the draw.

Of course there were always poachers like my friend Henry. But for the sake of discussion, let's give it a starting point. Let's say that it goes as far back as the Black Law of 1723. This was when the middle class was starting to rise, and being very protective about their little piece of the pie. A law was passed to protect them from poachers who in the previous centuries would be able to take a deer or two, or a fish or two, from the master's land or ponds without commotion. It changed with the arrival of the liberalized gentry, who did not see this with such favour. So men poaching (the Black Law was so called because these men would camouflage themselves in black faces) were not only fined and jailed, but hanged as well.

And those who poached challenged this law very bravely, with their lives, because to them some fundamental principle of fair play was at stake: All the game should not be for gentlemen when my child is starving at home.

Though there is now less starvation and almost no gentlemen, the contest between these two groups is still an ongoing one. I see it on every river I fish, and every time an animal falls from a poacher's rifle. The rules are still the same as well, as too is the deceit and the accusations of one group or the other.

It is only the animals that suffer. The animals become a commodity, or a political flashpoint. And once something becomes a commodity, or a political weapon, there is no end of nefarious backbiting and greed involved.

To me there is nothing worse than seeing a fish fight a jig hook. It is a three-pronged barb a person will put on the end of their line and toss into a pool where fish are lying, and then jig the barb upwards to catch the fish under the belly or along the back. You can tell when a fish is on a jig because of how crazily they run in the water. It demeans fishing in a way few other things do.

Laws do not work if a white poacher believes in his mind that Indians have a certain favouritism because of who they are.

Certainly the fish, the salmon, becomes the fodder. Like most other political weapons, the real reason why it is used becomes in the end obscured and demeaned.

The Miramichi can become a war zone in the summer. A war zone over the great fish who have no idea of the part they play. Sometimes the war is just a few skirmishes with disgruntled fishermen. On other times it is an all-out confrontation between whites and Indians, the federal Fishery Department, and the RCMP.

But so many of the poachers I know believe rightly or wrongly (and all of them have a case) that the laws were made by and for the king's men, and not for them. So I return to the Black Law of 1723. They believe they are the ones left out of the equation. And so too were their fathers and grandfathers and his father before him. And if we look closely at this, it usually has some validity. To a poacher, the salmon or moose becomes a political weapon in a battle with other human beings, who have no other political weapons left to use. In all cases it is the salmon that suffer. Any other view is hauling the wool over our own eyes.

The sports fisherman or woman must know they play a part in this, and sometimes there is resentment towards them, because they are looked upon with a special favour. The government wishes to attract them to the river with the ideas of pristine wilderness and abundant game. And many of the places on the river are out of reach, for one reason or another, to the average person living on it.

Society is usually unfair and the warden becomes seen as the arbitrator of unfairness, a parcelled-out unfairness, that deems certain people more acceptable in certain areas on the water than others. The law will always favour some more than others.

So a few fish are taken, or a few too many fish, or a few deer or moose out of season. These things always have a tendency to escalate. And then it becomes a game within a game of which poacher can outwit the other.

Also I should mention that I have seen the grandeur of some of the camps that others have never gotten to, and have listened at times to the ribald idiocy of wealthy or privileged people, who could fish in pools which those I have loved could never come near to. Then you think of the British commoner and what he must think of the blood sporting of the nobility.

One camp I stayed in had flourished in the age of the king's men, in the age of princes and princelings who had grown up on the fox hunt and had brought their trophies over to Canada as a testament to their privilege. The heads of water buffalo and the skins of lions, the hand of a gorilla as an ashtray and the foot of an elephant for a garbage can.

There was no way we could fish near those pools that their successors did, unless we were invited in for half an afternoon. When one time a friend of mine and I were invited there, he was like a child.

"My God," he said. "The water—have you ever seen such beauty in the water."

"I want to show you where the fish are," the guide said. My friend looked over the water, squinting his eyes.

"Oh, I know where the fish are," he said. And went out and hooked two that morning.

The people who had been there just before we arrived had flown in their private jet to New York for brunch. My friend had yet to be in a plane.

Such are the monumental gaps in the fishing life that the New Brunswick infomercials about conservation never seem to get.

That year, the year I fished on the Bartibog with Peg, I went hunting along the Fundy coast. I came across, at different times, two small graveyards of Irish immigrants who had died during the hard winters of the 1850s.

They were buried and their communities disappeared, and they were left for eternity to themselves. One day I came across Mary and Jacob Kelly, lying alone in the middle of nowhere, having died in 1858.

One night, just at dark, after waiting on deer in the snow well beyond the road towards the craggy shore of Fundy Bay, I made my way back to the truck, and came across Mary McGregor's family. Her children and she were there, under a granite stone, and a pair of angel's wings covered with moss. I stopped to look at the writing and heard the far-off rattle of a buck.

I made my way back out to the truck in the dark, and the next morning went in early. Just at dawn I walked down to the shore where the deer had been moving. The bay was frothy and cold, the swells calm and deceptive. It is a huge bay, terrible for its cold and rich in sea life. Hardly a fisherman from the shore of Fundy who goes to fish knows how to swim, although they walk back and forth on eight-inch gunnels from bow to stern. What would be the point in knowing how to swim when the temperature of the water would take you under in two or three minutes?

I made my way through the woods and sat down to wait. The day, except for a visit from an occasional moose bird and the chatter of a squirrel, was lonely and quiet.

At quarter to five that night a huge deer stepped out of the thicket of spruce just below me.

I was to lose that deer not by a poor shot but because the wardens decided I didn't have the proper tags. I don't think I've ever been *more* infuriated with authority in my life.

Although they gave the deer back later—took the hide off and cut the meat for me, because it was their mistake—it ruined the deer season, and what I had gone through to get it. It was the first and only time I thought seriously of poaching a deer. I got up one morning at five o'clock and drove along the back road between Sussex and Saint Martin. There, just at daybreak, I saw a little four-point buck standing in the ditch in front of my headlights.

Well, I couldn't do it. I put the clip away and went home.

Although I was not going to hunt again the next year, the second last week of the season I took my rifle and drove north. Spurred by the idea that I would have a good hunt, and that I would get a buck, and that there would be no mix-up in my credentials. I hunted for two days and on the third the snow started to fall.

That third day I saw one deer but couldn't get a shot at it. I don't know if it was a small buck or a doe. But going in towards the beaver dam I saw the scrape of a very large buck, which I couldn't have missed by more than fifteen minutes.

I waited until dark but the snowstorm was getting very bad, and I drove out to my father's house. I started to pack, to leave for Saint John the next morning. Then I thought that I would give it one more chance. It would be the last chance I would have to hunt.

So I set the clock and got into bed.

When I woke I heard my father shouting out to me: "You can't go hunting in this."

I looked out the window and it was almost blizzard conditions.

"I'll give it a try," I said.

I started off in my four-wheel drive, my windshield wipers slapping away, and rubbing the fog from the window every few minutes. I parked the truck on the side road I wanted, and everything was getting worse. I took my rifle and walked the mile or so into the small backfield where the buck had been crossing. The trees were waving and wind was howling. Halfway into the field I saw the buck's shoe-size slur of tracks on the road. I went up to the place I had stood for most of the hunt and waited.

But it was impossible. Even if he was circling towards me, I would be frozen by the time he got there. My teeth were chattering and my fingers were swollen numb.

"Dammit," I said, after an hour, and I put my rifle over my shoulder and started towards the truck. I had not gone twenty yards when the big buck stepped out in front of me and stood still.

I had a long way to go with the deer, and it was a hard pull. So I went back to the truck to get some rope, and then decided to give Peter a call. He came with a friend and helped me bring it out, a nine-point buck, 220 pounds. It was the last time I seriously hunted. And it is not that important to me if I ever hunt again.

Fifteen

THE NEXT YEAR I WAS on the river early. I went black salmon fishing for the first time, which is fun, but I can't get too excited about it. They are salmon that have wintered up under the ice and are backing out into the bay. They are voracious and skinny and not very great fighters, although they are certainly well worth fishing. Some people used to do all their fishing in the black salmon season and fillet the fish to fry them. But I would far rather fish the bright lads coming in.

It was now my eighteenth year fishing and I had learned much. I still have much to learn, but I knew when the fish would take. I knew what pools to fish and when to fish them and I was no longer subject to worry about whether I could get fish or not. I had done it.

I have fished with some excellent casters— Wayne Curtis, and his sons, Jason and Jeff—and realize that success depends a good deal on consistency to throw a line in the right way and right measure cast after cast.

I had some fun times learning this. I used to try and expend too much line, and cast well beyond the fish, or for the life of me I couldn't *get* to the fish.

But it is all in the presentation and the fly. You have to know which fly to use, in high water, in low, and all the levels in between. On a bright or cloudy day, you usually adjust to the colour around you.

Yet at times a big fly works in very low warm water.

One day at a pool on the Norwest with my wife's uncle, Bill Savage, we had fished every fly we could. It was in the middle of July and we had walked in a long way. By midday it was very warm. The sun was hot and high, the water was low. Both of us had been through three pools about five times, and we were tired of moving back and forth. Each pool was separated by flat water a quarter mile apart, and each pool was now dead and warm—and there wasn't another fisherman on the river.

By that time, with the walk in, and the fishing, we had

covered about eight or nine miles. I lay on the rocks of the shore with my waders in the water.

My wife's uncle pointed just below the rocks towards the middle of the pool.

"There's fish there," he said.

He rummaged about his fly box and took out a fly—a large Mickey Finn streamer that he used for black salmon fishing in April.

"What in hell are you after—marlin?"

"We'll see—I'm goin' big."

"Come big or stay home," I said shaking my head.

He tied on his Mickey Finn. Then he walked out. He started at the top of the pool and worked his way along. When his fly reached my side of the rock and just started to make its arc, into the run that widened out into the larger part of the pool, I saw a splash and his line tighten.

"Here it is," he said matter-of-factly, looking over at me, as if he knew all along that this would happen. I heard the singing of the reel, and stood to get a look at the fish.

I could not believe it. The grilse took a run and jumped. It was well hooked, and not accidentally jigged by the tail as I thought might have happened. My wife's uncle looked carefully at it as it jumped the second time, and then he began to work it towards shore.

The fly I dislike the most which I have gotten fish on is the Green Machine, a green bug with a light-brown hackle. I have talked to the three fishermen I respect the most and all of them admit to the same aversion. They hate it but they keep it in their box because they know it is productive. This is a strange anomaly within a fisherman's life. For if you dislike a fly, you'll rarely take a fish on it.

The one fly I do love is a stiff-winged butterfly with a green butt. A fairly common fly to be sure, but a great fly to work a pool with. I love a Silver Doctor as well, and any fly with some silver on the body is bound to attract my attention, even if it doesn't attract the fish.

Far upriver one day on the open water of the elbow stretch on the Norwest Miramichi, a small Green Butt Butterfly fell out of my box of flies when I was ready to put my rod away and walk back to the truck.

Was this an omen? Well, I don't have a clue. But fishermen certainly think of things like this, as omens. So I put it on and began to work my way into the water again.

I had fished this section on the way up and had seen nothing, but running the river the year before with friends we had picked up two fish here, and I cast over towards the left bank, watched my fly work towards the middle of the run, and felt my line jerk.

I brought the grilse in, in the rain, and backed up stepping on Roo's feet, so that she let out a terrible wail. The fish looked as if it had just come into the river.

I made it along the path with Roo and found my truck, and my tire flat. Again I was without fly dope, and I had left my adrenaline needle at my father's. Trying to find a place to put the jack up against the rusted body of my old truck was a job, and worse, I was trying to jack up in muck, so I had to find some rocks. Then it took me an hour or more—with some kicking and screaming—to get the spare tire down, and when I put it on, it was almost as flat as the tire I had just taken off.

Then I piled Roo in the truck and started off. I was halfway home when I remembered my fish, lying on the grass where I had first discovered my predicament.

I'm a bugger for fun, so back I went, and at ten o'clock that night found the fish, and turning about again, started for home.

"I know how to take a shortcut to the pool," Peter says. It is late June and the water is still cool and high. We have started out in the early morning to walk to a pool a few miles away. But Peter explains that there is a better way to get there.

Peter takes a compass reading and we head off, wearing waders and fishing vests, carrying rods and a hatchet straight into the fly-infested woods—half foolhardy and more ambitious than we will be later on.

We hit an old logging road. The trees are just beginning to wave slightly, silently above us. Come to an old bridge, torn apart at least two generations before by ancestors of both he and I.

"Just over there," he said, "I'm sure."

I was not so sure. I tried to hear the river. Look at the sky, the dip of the land, and you can tell. Couldn't tell.

This was not a new experience for Peter and me at that time. We had done this often in those years a while ago. Sooner or later we'd find ourselves in the middle of a bog, searching for a distant pool, where we knew the fish had moved into the night before—or were perhaps just moving into now.

That's the thing. They are always there.

There is always a better forest path to the spring, as the great writer and unrepentant drunk Malcolm Lowry knew, that will bring you out to the pool, easier and quicker than ever before.

In the bog, walking towards a sparkling river in the mid-June heat is one side of the equation.

Then there is the other side of fishing.

Sitting at a dinner in Montreal one night an influential man making small talk told me we had something in common.

"We both fish," he said.

"Fly-fish," I said.

"Yes," he said. "I do okay. Take my jet down to New Brunswick every year. Spend about fifteen hundred dollars at the camp, have my guide meet me, you know—I get my fish. It's relaxing. I like it. Like to hear their stories. The old guides have great stories, you know—and its surprising how smart they can be. Takes my mind off this." And he waved his hand at the palatial room.

Perhaps he wouldn't understand that I had a good deal of sympathy for him at that moment.

There is always the big fishing trip Peter and I are going to go on also. Win the Lotto. Go to Labrador. Bone fishing down south. As long as it's a fly rod.

I've heard fishing described as Zen. Most of the people I know as fishermen wouldn't know Zen. Fishing has its *own* language. Like great hockey, it manages to be an act in itself. And of course, beyond all the pleasant afternoons beside a pool, narrowing to a fine rip, and the sometimes naive, ethereal descriptiveness, fishing is finally about Green Butts, Copper Killers, Rusty Rats, low-water bugs, Green Machines, blood and death.

Remembering this, it becomes no different than waxing eloquent about hunting or bull fighting.

Taking roe out of a hen fish that has fought you to its death for twenty minutes is just a difference in degree from gutting and taking the hide off a doe whose spine you shattered with your .306 on a logging road one November afternoon.

I say this only because of those I've met who, while talking in poetic psycho-babble about fly-fishing, have clamoured to stop the bestiality of the moose hunt.

Having done both, I don't think the fly-fisherman has an iron-clad case.

We were in the woods, the flies black about us, swimming in and out of my great big ears.

"I don't know—think we're turned about," Peter said. "Any fly dope?"

"Never wear it," I said.

We lit a smoke and watched the trees.

Thinking the river was much closer, we had not trusted the compass. So here we were, sitting in the heat of mid-morning, in the middle of a fly-infested bog.

"Well, we can't stay here."

"I'm going to finish my smoke," I said.

Actually the arthritis in my foot was paining and I didn't think I could walk for a while. All this for a fish.

"The thing is we're not trusting the compass. Trust the compass and we'll get back out to the logging road," he said.

I know a man who once owned his own surveying company, and had to make himself dizzy—literally close his eyes and turn in a circle until he fell down. Then not knowing what direction west or east was, he would finally *have* to rely on his compass. It was at this moment I knew why.

Anyway, sweat pouring down, we took another reading and found we were going in exactly the wrong direction. Even then, we hesitated to believe it.

Once we decided to believe it we were back on the logging road in ten minutes. But the morning was gone.

"All this for a fish," my friend said.

But fishing is still fishing. And what people do for it still shows you what it's worth.

One blowsy day in mid-July and David Savage had had enough of salmon fishing and was looking through his box of trout flies. He drove far up the Bartibog and parked his car under the giant spruce with the lightning mark. It was coming onto twilight. Just when others were going home. He walked through the woods to the pool. He had put his salmon rod away, and had his little trout rod with him. The air had turned still and smelled of rain.

He started downriver, flicking his small bug under the alders. Soon he had one trout, and then two. It was growing dark. He knew he should turn back, find the path. But as he was playing a fish, he saw a trout break water at the bottom of a pool far downriver.

That's a big fish, he thought. And he moved towards it.

He reached the pool, shortened up his cast, and worked his way to it. On the fourth cast the fish came and he felt the line tighten.

The air was still, and it was almost dark. It was a big trout too, about four pounds. He managed to net it after a time. But it was dark. Only the water glimmered milkily. Far off he saw the very top of the spruce tree he had parked his car under.

He decided to cut through the woods. He broke down his rod and put his fish in the knapsack. He started up the hill.

By the time he reached the top of the hill it had started to rain heavily. It was dark. And it was only then did he realize that it wasn't the same spruce, the one with the lightning mark.

He would have to go back to the river.

It was so dark he took his rod tip and began to feel the trees so he wouldn't lose an eye. And he made his way along silently as the rain pitter-pattered the leaves. He knew reaching the river he could make his way back to the path. But before he did this he fell. All of a sudden his legs went, and he found himself tumbling into a pit half-filled with water.

He climbed up one side and sat on a ridge.

"Well, I don't know which direction I fell, or where the river is now—I'm here for the night."

He sat in the pulverizing rain and waited.

He sat for over two hours in the same spot. It was almost midnight. And then far off he heard the sound of a transport on the highway.

Ah, he thought. The highway was to his right. His car then must be to his left. He would inch his way left until he found the path. And with this in mind, and taking his rod tip, he started out again.

Little by little he inched along the hill, the water far below him. He walked in the dark for almost an hour.

And suddenly he noticed an animal in front of him.

Too big for a deer or coyote; it was either a bear or a moose. But he couldn't tell. It was still raining and the black shape stood in front of him. There was now only one thing to do. Hit it with his rod tip—scare it away. He took a deep breath.

"Go on," he said, snapping it.

It was his car.

I am down at Dr. Wilson's fishing through for the second time in the morning. The sun is now above the tree line, and the day ticks with the scent of coming heat.

I have raised a fish too, and have seen another jump—it may have been the same fish. I haul out a chew of plug, and spit and watch the water as it swirls about my waders.

"Thirty of them dead, thirty more gone." I think suddenly about a poem I have written about my friends. I suppose it is strange to think this way when the day is nice and you are having a fish, but then who said I wasn't strange. Maybe the fish think this way about each other. Who's to say.

I have put on a Bear Hair and wade far above the rocks. The water is high but not too much, and is dropping now, and mild-coloured leaves swirl away in the eddies. I lean against the boulder in back of me, and feel the heat on my face, and watch the light and spray as the water runs to rapids just below.

I let my line relax in the water and stare off at the morning haze, and then up at a plane skimming so high above me that I cannot hear it for moments, and then only as a distant drone.

My friend Peter is working. He'll be off in the next few days and we'll go up again—one more time to the south branch of the Sevogle.

We will once again put the canoe in at Clearwater or Simpson and move out in the early morning to fish.

As I am thinking this, still standing in Wilson's Pool, a

canoe comes around the corner with two men and a boy. The men are two old mossy-backed charlatans of my youth. They don't recognize me, as I them. We are all bearded, midsummer tanned, and they are shouting wildly to one another about the rapids, and about tipping the canoe.

Then they pull in just above me. I start in again, and fish down, but their canoe is pulled up so it is hard to cast. So I let my line slacken and wait. The taller of the men takes the little boy and starts across the river, wading into the rapids above me, like an old moose with her young.

The man leaves the child on the rock directly above the heaviest rapid, at the widest part of the river, and continues on across—to effectively move down and cut me off from the fish I saw roll. But I can't move.

I feel obligated to stay with the child. I don't know whose child it is—it is not mine—but sitting in the middle of the river, with thirty pounds of waders on, and weighing no more than forty-five pounds himself, it seems that he is an easy drowning victim.

As I am deciding what to do, the second man, who has finished his beer at a walk, now enters the river just below me, which is about the height of bad manners—and really I can't think of much worse. Perhaps killing a man in his sleep, and then calling it bravery.

He looks back at me and says, "Well, you weren't fishin'—you were waitin'."

There are incidents like this on the Miramichi also. Thank God they are not as many as the pleasant ones.

Sixteen

IT IS THE SUMMER OF 1995. And now once more we are going to find the fish. Again the water is moving unconcerned with us, with those who have come before, and with those who will come after. To the water we are all the same. Once again the water is the right temperature and the day is sky-high and cool, and my friend Peter and I put the canoe in at Clearwater and make our way out into the South Branch, past the rocks, and skirting the trees that come from ancient sources. Away we go, searching the rocks and crevices where the water swirls, moving to the rhythms of moving water under it we cannot see. The rocks of Karnak one might think of, or that each rock is like a jutting Sphinx made by the hand of God, amended by the weather which is the breath of God, and giving sound to the water, which is the voice of God. And this voice is the life of God. We see the rips and eddies where fish were taken ten years before, we remember the hour and the day, the kind of wind, and the kind of fight the fish gave, where it lay, and how it was hooked, the sunlight upon it that has disappeared into the universe once more.

And all along on this dry cool day we are looking for fish, who are as much the children of God, as we. In the green hillsides ancient trees watch us pass, muted, and life goes on about them, the trembling squirrel that chatters at us, or the soaring osprey.

"Remember the bog in there," Peter says once we are down a ways.

"The bog where I got caught up to my waist," I say.

"I brought George down through there one day," Peter says. "I wanted to fish Disappointment Pool. I wanted to have a nice fish with my dog. My dog would sit beside me, and I would catch a large salmon. But it didn't work that way. As soon as I got to the pool George picked up a scent and took off after a deer. I couldn't go after him because I had hooked a grilse. You know where—that little rip halfway along in the pool."

"What were you using?"

"Bug."

Peter told me that it was a perfect day. But there are no real perfect days any more, and perhaps there never have been. I have been left a child in thinking of them, or searching for them. I have not found them, even on the mystic river far from the sounds of man. We are the only creatures who as a part of life are never satisfied with it.

Peter had to land the grilse before he could start to hunt for George.

"I cursed poor old George that afternoon," he said.

"I curse this river," I answer. "I curse it every day of my life—I curse coming in here now—I curse it because I know it. I know this is my last chance until the fall for fishing. I know when I am down in here it is a hard pull. Because we will have to pull the canoe halfway along. And halfway along we will decide we will have to go somewhere else, to the place all the fish really are. And that you will begin to plan fishing trips in your mind that are more complex than the equation for noncombustible fusion."

"But of course you love it too," Peter said. And that was true enough as well. I loved every river I was on, and every slap of water that cut my waders or my jeans, and even in the end the damnable flies. But now, with children at home, it seemed somehow lonelier, and so far away.

So that day, long ago, Peter put the grilse in a bed, placed his rod near a tree, and made his way along the river path, overgrown and mined with stones and pitfalls, to find his dog. He found the dogs tracks a mile down along the shore, on a small piece of tough sand along the beach.

That moment, too, has passed into eternity. This is what happens. Each moment on the river passes into eternity in the blink of an eye. The moments just disappear. The echoes of the water become the longing babbles of ghosts at twilight.

"I walked down to Island Pool for the dog," he said. "And I was both perturbed and compressed over that animal. I stared at Island Pool—and noticed that it was full of fishes."

"*Muchas pescado,*" I answered in Spanish.

And Peter continued on:

"And here I was without my rod. I remembered the first salmon I ever took there twenty years before—did I tell you about that?"

"Oh yes," I said.

"Are you ever going to write about that?" Peter asked.

"I don't know."

"I bet you'll never mention getting sucked up in the bog that first year," Peter laughed.

"Probably not," I said.

And we tipped about another corner, a river spined with rocks, and a jet trail far above us in the heavens.

"You will not write about getting your line all tangled up in that tree, when I snuck that picture of you."

"Perhaps not," I said.

"Or missing the buck that time because you knocked your sights."

"Perhaps not."

"Or having no sense of direction in the woods—so Savage and I had to haul you by your feet out through it or you'd die with bug imbalance like you got a few years ago."

"Bug imbalance," I laugh. "Perhaps I won't mention that."

So Peter watched the fish at Island Pool and smoked a cigarette and stared at the lonely river. And no George. He called to it for a long time, and it was getting later in the day.

"Finally I decided I had to go home without him. And in order to prepare for this I cursed him down to the ground. Let him get lost—let him get eaten by the great Miramichi wood slough, I didn't care."

"But you did care."

"Of course not," Peter said, lying. "I didn't care."

He started out. He walked back to Disappointment Pool and gathered his fishing rod and his grilse, waded the rapid at the top of it and cut into the woods on his right and then made his way up the steep almost indecipherable path towards his truck, stopping and calling the dog at various points along the way, while searching for his ribbon marking. But no George.

He drove back home.

"Where's George?" Nicki asked.

"Damned if I know," he said.

"Well, then," he continued his story, "Nicki and the kids started worrying and made me worry, poor George was going to get eat by something and I was cruel. So I couldn't stand it, and had to get back into the truck, take my flashlight, and go all the way back into this godforsaken place, down over that godforsaken hill, and try to find George. At night in the dark—with the big bears and stuff."

He combed the area again, with the flashlight in the dark. He shone the light on the trees at the opposite side of the river and walked all the way down to Island Pool once more.

"But no George," I said.

"No George," he answered.

So back home he went exhausted, muddied wet, and tired. Into the dooryard he comes, opens the porch door, and lo and behold George, lying on his mat, wagging his tail. Happy as a clam to see him.

"Three lads in here fishing found him wandering about, and realized it was my dog and brought him home. Mind you,

I didn't have to speak too loud to get the kids to do any chore, the next few days."

So we are on the river again, and I'm thinking of why we try to use the metaphor of God when describing it. Perhaps there is nothing else to describe it as. Norman Maclean in *A River Runs Through It* did it best, but Faulkner and Hemingway did it well too, and I think that perhaps in fly-fishing there is an element of combating unknown forces of life with such a small line, such minute precisely tied flies, that there is no other way to ever describe it. But still, in some way it leaves us at a loss for words. For once you describe something as God, there is nothing else you can describe it *as*.

We pass the big dead water hole. The salmon come up into this stretch of the river and hug hard the far bank, where they rest aside hidden boulders under the river. You fish a dry fly or a bug and you can see them swirl as they chase it while you strip line. But they are hard to interest here, and today they are uninterested. We beach the canoe and walk up along this bank.

Now, today, this river, this place far away from the world at large, is my home. I know the rock I sat upon last summer at this same time—and seven summers before that. And I think of the little girl sitting near Dennis Pool the day I went out for fiddleheads, drinking her hot chocolate, and wonder what she is doing, and that she is now a teenager.

I know how the path is overgrown, and I step to my right automatically, without thinking now, because I know one step to the left will make me slide on the greasy mud into the deep water hole itself. But of course I myself am becoming just one more ghost while I remember this. I too am disappearing on this river, like that little girl drinking the hot chocolate, and I can see myself as a younger man fading into the past, on every turn we take.

I've always had my battles. Most of them were with myself. Falling against a hard rock one day and cracking a rib, but refusing to let go of my rod. A rib on my left side. And then my brother cracking a rib on my right side, in a friendly tussle, with a left hook. So I went to the doctor to get a checkup before I left for England where one of my books was being published, and the doctor said I had spots on my lungs. And he wanted to check them for malignancy. So they put me through a number of tests, and when I went back he told me that the spots weren't in my lungs but on ribs that had healed, from being cracked or broken. I don't know if I was happy or disappointed, because I'd already begun to make out my will, but at least the excitement was over.

Four salmon are resting here, today, under the shaded water, behind the orange-black boulders. They look so intent on making it to wherever they are going. It seems in a way that the entire world is against them. It is amazing to see them torpedo through this water with such infinite strength. They have come in past the factory ships, the drifters, the mills soaking the water in pollution and rinse, the filth from the sewers, the nets on the reserves, the pitchforks and nets and jig hooks of Henry the Poacher, and are not yet done their journey. They have miles and miles of river to go.

We both fish over them for a time, and though one moves up, and now and again shows interest, they all finally act as if we don't exist, or the flies we are presenting don't exist.

It is days like this that to me make the river great.

But Peter is complaining that this river is dead, compared to how it used to be. Yet it still stretches before us, unconcerned with anyone's assessment of it.

The trees are in full summer now, and the sky is wide open, and the bends of the river have let go of their early swell and become steady and regular. Peter is now a grandfather, though he is a man in his early forties, and those children of his that I held as infants long ago have grown to young womanhood.

It seems an amazing irony that he wouldn't have boys, but he takes the girls into the woods with him whenever he gets a chance. And they will have every opportunity to hunt or fish if they desire.

We push on to Island Pool and fish it, with the wind just slight on our backs. And we talk of other men who have been in here, and of a trip we made once long ago, when we walked the entire afternoon to get to this pool, and turned in the dark and started back. But we were younger and far more ambitious then.

Just above Island Pool is where David Savage came to hunt one year. There were men at various points *still* hunting up on the road, and he knew he wouldn't have much luck. The day was bitter and cold, with an inch or two of raw snow, and he went into the woods and walked down to the first embankment and waited, at about this point above the river. His hands were so frozen he could hardly open his thermos, and just as he poured a coffee, the largest buck he had ever seen came up over that embankment after crossing the river. He shot it, and began to lug it uphill a half a mile; it weighed three hundred and four pounds.

"I was winded at the end," he said.

Yes, there are deer in here, and whenever we fished we talked of hunting, and when hunting fishing. Perhaps it is a peculiar way to always be somewhere else, and to never be satisfied.

You try to think of how this river must have looked five

hundred years ago. And then we get into the canoe and try to navigate the rocks as one would a minefield.

it is summer yet but still the cold
coils through these fields at dusk

I think of that line from an early poem of Alden Nowlan. The day *is* cool but the sun has warmed us, and the spray from the water washes over the gunnels and hits our hands.

I can do all right on this river now, and other rivers also. And the one thing you learn—perhaps the most important thing of all—is to take your time. For time is infinite, and everything is preordained. Never mind the scoff that will come when this is said. A year on the river, ten years on the river will tell you how true this is. You will meet an animal at the exact moment you were supposed to—see it in the way the sun hits it, form an impression of it, and its destiny, and its link to you.

I tell Peter that my brother and I ran the Padapedia. It took us three days, and we caught a fish apiece.

"So this isn't the only hard river," I say.

Peter now is once again telling me the story of falling into the bear's lap. The water glistens coolly against us as he speaks.

"Bears," Peter says, finishing up his story and lighting a cigarette.

All stories blend into one another on the river, on the water, and become like the drone of some music, so it doesn't matter how many familiar variations one hears.

And I remember the bear with her cub, and the two stories related to me in the past year about seeing bears.

And it seems I should tell Peter about them. So I do.

One was about a woman, who is a good fisherwoman and a good hunter. She was up on the Dungarvon one morning with her husband. They had parked the truck on an old woods road and cut through the trees and across a blueberry field to the water. Then they walked up a ways to the pool she was going to fish, while her husband decided to travel further on.

"I'll be back in a couple of hours," he said to her. "Good luck."

It was a great morning for fishing. The water was dropping and the sky was clearing off, the patches of sun burning away the mist. Everything was quiet as she walked into the water and began to cast.

But suddenly she felt she was being watched.

"I thought my husband had come back," she said. "I had this strange feeling, and turned. There four yards behind me were three bears. A mother and two cubs about a year old. The mother grunted, sniffed the air, and tossed her head, but the cubs just jumped into the water. I waded out as far as I could, and then clamoured up on a rock. It was the only place I could go. I couldn't get to the truck and didn't want to start yelling for my husband."

For well over an hour she stood in the same position, as the bears walked, waded, and splashed all about her. Suddenly the mother gave a half heist up to her feet, turned sideways, and ran with the cubs behind her. Five minutes later her husband came sauntering down the beach.

"What in hell are you doing standing in the middle of the river on a rock?" he said. "You should be fishing over that rock, not standing on top of it."

"Bears," she said, "bears."

"Hell, darlin', they'll never bother you," he said.

But she was the one out in the river with them.

The other incident happened to a man I know who was spending the afternoon clearing some brush far from his camp, along the Renous with a friend. They were in a hurry because they wanted to finish and fish in the evening, and talked about fishing as they worked. They could hear the water—and what they were doing is clearing a lot of brush to make it easier for them to travel back and forth.

"I wasn't paying attention to what I was doing—I was only thinking of fishing. The axe glanced and cut my calf almost to the bone," he said.

His friend wrapped the wound, and said that he would have to go and get the truck at the camp, and come back in on the woods road that skirted the area they were clearing because it was too far for the fellow to walk.

The man hobbled over to a stump and waited, looking down at a small valley towards the river. He sat on the stump about fifteen minutes trying not to move, which would start the wound bleeding again.

Well, I won't get fishing now tonight, he thought. After a while he saw a male bear about two hundred yards away. The bear couldn't see him, but was sniffing and moving its head side to side.

"I didn't think this looked very good," the fellow said. "I waited for the bear to get a scent of me, and turn away, but I think what he got the scent of was my blood. I slapped my hands to scare it, but he kept wagging his head aggressively and coming towards me up that small hill. I waited until he was about twenty yards from me, and gave a loud cough. The bear grunted and kept coming. So I looked about. Behind the stump was a small tree—but any tree bigger I would have to run to. So I took my chances and climbed the one that was there. The bear came right up to the stump, sniffed it, and then came over to the tree and leaned up against it, looking up at me. I was about as high as I could go, only three feet from its paws, and the little tree was bending. So I was looking about for another tree. Then I decided to give a shout. I shouted at the top of my voice. This scared the bear badly and it went about fifteen feet sideways in a second, landed on its feet, threw out a paw and snapped a good-sized sapling up by its roots and far into the air as if it were a twig. Then it started to come back. The thing was, it walked over the brush we had piled that morning and made no sound at all. My axe was in the dirt by the stump. I was in a bad position, because the bear was very interested, and I was again bleeding badly.

"It got to the tree again, and leaned against it looking up at me. And then it heard the sound of the truck and took off, and was gone. So I got to the hospital all right, but couldn't fish much for the rest of the summer. I put it all in the log at the camp."

Some day we will stop travelling this river, I tell Peter. We will stop travelling all rivers. I never thought of this when I was four years old fishing Beaverbrook, and caught my first plump trout, and lost my sneakers and walked home with my socks in my pocket. I did not think of things that way. It was through a glass darkly, not unlike the beery brown water.

But I think now that some day it will just not be worth it to us any more, and we will not put the canoe in at Simpson's or at the Miner's Bridge. And we too will become like Mr.

Simms holding up in his shaking fingers his beautiful Copper Killer, while sitting in the kitchen of his house. And others will be here and call the rivers their own.

Each bridge we cross in the summer, we stop the truck, get out and walk over to the edge to look down at the pool below to count the grilse. We often think there are fewer fish now than there used to be, although that might not be true. My uncle, Richard Adams, said in an interview a few years back that there are as many salmon now as there ever were. But perhaps that is wishful thinking. No one can stare at a river, hear the slough of a paddle coming upon you in the evening, listen to the laughter of men and women who have lived by and have loved these waters, without being hopeful.

We talk of conservation as we take fish and talk of taking fish when we are at a meeting about conservation.

But this bridge spotting has gone on now for almost twenty years, and I can truthfully say I can actually see grilse or salmon below those bridges in those pools. It takes a while to be able to discern their shape, so blended are they, so part of their world they are.

I want my son to get a fish, and last year we went up to the Souwest with my friend, writer and guide, Wayne Curtis. However, though he didn't catch one, hope springs eternal, and next year we will go again. We will spend days on the river, I tell my son, and we will fry fish over an open fire on the beach, and canoe too. We will do all the things that I wanted to do as a boy and never got a chance. But again I suppose life is like a spiral, and things have to be done, and traded, and bartered for. And one of those things is time. And I see myself, like my father before me, stuck in an office and travelling to Toronto, and there is always a moment when children break your heart, because they run into the room to tell you something so important to them, and you're not there.

We pass Two Mile Pool, where I have never taken a fish from, and Peter gets out and throws a line. I see it arcing above him in perfect balance, and the fly jotting against the small ripples. Far up the hill is where we used to park our truck. The road now is all overgrown and swamped, and new roads cut through the silence. On this cool day the wind is beginning to move the trees up on the slopes, and I hear the chatter of a squirrel far away.

Peter hooks a little grilse.

Some give a Miramichi whoop when they hook a fish. I used to the first few years. I no longer do.

Peter never speaks. So you look at his line moving across the water, turn away for a moment, look again, and his rod is bowed, and he has switched hands.

"How did that take?"

Peter shakes his head.

"Not very well. Move the canoe up so I can come in there," he says, but as soon as he does the line goes limp. He looks over and slaps his line.

"It's gone," he says. He brings his line in and searches for his bug, looks at it a moment, breaks it off with his teeth, and reties it. He smiles as he sees the little grilse flop in the water a few feet from him.

"Hurt fish won't take," he says.

Although that is normally true, it is not consistently the truth. Once on the Little Souwest I had a hit that must have hurt the fish, and simply as a reaction threw the fly right back at it, and it took hard again, and I managed to land it. Often on this river on a slow day, we will ask ourselves what in God's name are we doing. But this day, though a slow day, never brings this to mind.

In his camp, at night, Peter will begin to talk about the rivers he is going to fish the next day. And very soon he is travelling all the rivers of the Miramichi system in his mind. He will go from Gin Point on the Big Sevogle to the Norwest, to the Little Souwest, in a matter of seconds, mentioning the pools he has to fish, as if he is a wizard of some renown. And the best thing one can do with him at these points is just nod and say "Sure."

Now he is telling me another story interlaced and interwoven with another, to make it textured and respectable as a story of the woods should be.

He was hunting, and he had wounded a deer and lost his clip, and had to follow it for three miles, until he finally got another bullet into it.

"I felt sorry for that deer," he said, "because I lost my clip."

"That was up at Louis Lake," I say remembering that story, and he says that yes it was. All those years ago.

It was a strange thing that Louis Lake, far up on the Plaster Rock, he tells me.

He and a friend went fishing one day, thinking that there was arctic char there. It was a late spring day, and the ice had been out of the river for a month, but when they got to the lake it was covered in ice. So they found another lake, smaller and further away, which was ice-free, and they unhooked their boat and got rigged out and fished for three hours without any luck.

Then packing up their boat and rigging and heading back home, they passed Louis Lake once more.

"All the ice was gone," Peter said. "It was ice covered when we went in, and gone when we started out."

So in some amazement they got the boat off the trailer, got their rods, and rowed out to the middle to fish.

"It was the strangest thing," Peter said. "Looking down at the entire bottom, as far as we could see, was covered in a sheet of ice. All the ice in the lake had sunk in once gigantic piece, and killed the fish—who knows—but there was no arctic char there that day."

Coming in here on this day we had a surprise. The fishery officers pulled us over, and lo and behold, to my eternal amazement, out of the truck came Henry, my old poaching friend.

He checked our licences and tags for the numbers, signed our licenses, with the time and date, and made a cursory look about our truck and under our canoe. He was now a fish warden, and looked very professional, and somewhat put out and suspicious of us. Finally I caught his eye and said hello.

"How are you boys doin'?" he asked, looking up under the truck, which must have been a place he had once put poached fish himself.

"How long have you been a fish warden?" I ask.

"Oh, a long time now." He looks at me, as if in severe puzzlement that I would ask such a question.

He told me that old Mr. Simms had died. I hadn't seen him in a number of years, and I was always going to go back and say hello.

"He died on the river," he says. "His brother had to take him by wheelchair down to a pool. And he went to sleep there one afternoon last week. I don't think his brother will last very much longer now—they were twins, you see."

I was fishing on that day as well, on the main Souwest, and I think of this. Sometimes you will be startled by a death, because you had been thinking of that person that very day. Often it is like this. But I had not seen or thought of Mr. Simms in a while. And the last time I saw him, I believe, was the day I had taken him the fiddleheads.

Henry got into his truck and nodded to us, put it in gear and drove away, looking among the hills and torrents of our river system for lawbreakers who displeased him.

Paul, in *A River Runs Through It,* wanted to be the greatest fly-fisherman in the world. I know men who held on to the same dream. My friend, Rick Tretheway, wrote a poem called "Dreaming of Rivers," where he is always going back to the rivers of his youth, of his home, which is always somewhere else from where he now lives. But it is never the same as in your dreams. In our dreams we always float like the airborne angels above it, float like the pollen carried on the feet of bees, see it as it relates to our subconscious, where all decisions can be made in a second, and all decisions seem right.

In reality it pays at best an irregular dividend. The river can sap our energy as much as bring life to us. And I am passing the place I stood my second year of fishing, where I went down swinging at the air, with both fists, roundhouses at the bugs, after I had lost a fish. I remember Peter laughing so hard he almost fell into the water.

"Throw your jab," he was saying. "Step inside and hook that bug."

Now, remembering how I lost that fish, I am telling Peter, not that story, but another one, about my dog Jeb Stuart and me on the Little Souwest one summer day, years ago, fishing with my old heavy Fenwick. Jeb got caught in the rapid near Harris Brook, as I crossed, and down he went. I thought he had drowned. I couldn't see him for a minute or two and started to run along the shore trying to find him, ready to jump in and haul him out by the tail. But then I spotted him on the far side of the river, coming up along the bank. Before I got my old Fenwick together he had come across and was shaking himself off beside me as if he had performed a wonderful task I should be pleased with. Dogs, when they shake next to you, always seem to think a lot of themselves.

There is nothing like an old Fenwick today. The rod I use, a Loomis, has been given to me by the people of the Miramichi and I am proud of that fact. It is a supple rod, nine and a half feet long, and I have a nice reel now, which holds a good line. We are travelling the small short river again, in hope of the fish that will hold up in the pool, the fish that have travelled those thousands of miles to meet us, the progeny of fish we missed a few years before. And Peter is replete with stories and is telling me another one.

Peter tells his story about getting a truck stuck and it is as if I can see him and his friend working hour after hour to get the truck back up on the grade.

"I had to walk through to the highway," Peter said, "and didn't get back until late at night. So once we got the truck back up, I decided to stay in alone, and fish in the morning." He took a sleeping bag and went down over the hill and stretched out. The flies woke him at dawn.

"How did you make out?"

"I didn't see a fish," he laughs. "And I haven't had much luck on this river since—I have to try somewhere else. Fishing is getting harder on this river every year."

So I tell him that sometimes when fishing was hard, the old folks would capture a mouse and put it on a shingle, and float the shingle down the river. The mouse would sit upon the shingle because it didn't want to get wet, and then the fisherman would cast his line over the mouse and hook it. The mouse would jump off the shingle and start to swim for shore, and as often as not, a large salmon would break water below it, and swallow it.

"That's pretty hard on a mouse," Peter says.

Peter then told me he once hooked a duck in the water, and our friend, Doug Underhill, hooked a squirrel.

"I would never eat a fish I saw swallow a mouse," Peter said.

Another thing the old folks did on a hard day, I tell Peter, is that they would go up to the top of a pool and shovel some dirt into it. The dirt mixing with the flow of water would turn to silt, the fish would be fooled into thinking the water was rising and would start to take.

These stories were told me by Mr. Simms when I was twelve years old. When I was the little Christ child, who was supposed to become a fisher of men, and preach in the temple.

Peter asks me if I believe these stories, and I tell him I didn't know, but that something quite like these stories probably happened at one time or another. And of our friends at Allison run, who kick and scramble above the fish every year, to get them to take.

Then the talk trails off, as the trip becomes harder and more monotonous.

We haven't spoken in a long while and we are below Teacup Pool. The water is low and brown, so we are in and out of the canoe half a dozen times on a single stretch. My sneakers are water-soaked, and my jeans are soaked up to my thighs, and by now the canoe also needs to be bailed out. I am bruised by the rocks and from jumping in and out, and bitten by two hundred bugs.

"Do you remember the time on the Depo stretch when you lost your sneakers?" Peter asked.

Both the laces of my sneakers broke, and I had retied them a number of times. It was the third day of our fishing trip and we were walking way down to the pools, hoping to get some trout because it had been hard going with the salmon. Although, I must say, I had hooked a grilse earlier that morning, but I was looking back over my shoulder at the time and lost it. And I was looking back over my shoulder because Peter was telling me he knew for a fact that there were no fish in the pool, and I was telling him I had just seen one roll. When it took I wasn't ready and hauled the damn fly from its mouth.

"Oh God—you were right," Peter had said bending over with laughter.

So, I had lost my laces to my sneakers that day. The only thing we had left to tie my sneakers with was a bit of chain from Peter's compass. That didn't hold and I ended up walking barefoot back to the truck, over rocks and stumps, while Peter managed to make it down to a pool and hook a grilse. It reminded me again of my very first time fishing, at four years old, when I walked home with my socks in my pockets.

Today we will haul the canoe down to Three Minute Pool and fish it, and make it to White Birch by evening. Then we will sit out under the stars, and tomorrow we will make it down to the narrows where my truck is parked.

We pull up at Three Minute Pool and rest. I sit on a boulder in the sun and look at the water, dark and swift flowing against the cliff, and the trees' shade and shadow upon it. It has been almost twenty years since I first saw this pool.

"What are you using?" I ask Peter.

He doesn't answer. He steps out at the top of the pool, and the second cast he has a nice grilse. The grilse runs into the middle and sulks, butting his rod. Peter looks at me and starts to back in, but holds his ground as the grilse runs and jumps.

There is always a moment when I look away when a fish is having the life played from it.

The grilse turns along the ledge, and then cuts to its right, as if it wants to go over the rapids at the top of the pool. Then it turns back towards the centre but finds itself in shallow water, digging with all its strength to try to get back into the pool. It jumps again, and comes down in a rainbow just out from me, and Peter is to my right, and backs in and lands it.

He looks about.

"You know I have no picture of this pool, and I hardly have a picture of me on this river. Some day in winter, when I'm old, I'll try to remember what it all looked like. I'll have to come in here some day and get a picture."

I suppose I can say this, that the men I have been fortunate enough to know on the Miramichi generally do what they say they are going to do. There is no greater or finer gift in human nature than this. The men I admire the most are those who are most direct and unassuming about this. So then you should never tell a Miramichier you are going to kill him, because often as not he'll take you at your word.

I get some blades of grass and wet them to place over the grilse, and we move out.

It is late afternoon and there is only a little ways—five or six more turns—to White Birch. I look across the river and see myself walking up along the bank, up to my shoulders in grass, twenty years before. Peter, thinking this, says, "We must have been in awful good shape back then."

"And awful crazy."

We walked from White Birch all the way up to Two Mile Pool or beyond, and then would start back—and did this every day.

"And now we can afford the luxury of a canoe," Peter laughs.

The one thing about the Coleman canoe I own, it never minds how many rocks it goes over. And if you are on the south branch of the Sevogle River, you'd have to be blind not to hit a rock.

White Birch comes in view, and is calm and familiar in the evening air. The bugs are bad; the bugs are always bad so there is no use in mentioning it too much. We pull the canoe up on the beach, and begin to set up the tent. We light a small fire that is still transparent in the evening, and the smoke dissipates in the cooling air. I am shivering in my soaking jeans.

"Are we having that fish?" Peter says.

"No, no—you keep it."

Peter shrugs and starts to get it ready to cook.

I look through my fly box. There are some wonderful flies in it now. Undertakers, Squirrel Tails and Hairy Marys and bugs and Black Ghosts and more bugs—all will take fish. And I look and see the yellowish feather and black body and black hackle of my uncle Richard Adams favourite fly. The Black Dose. Something attracts me to it. And I try to remember where this fly came from and though, like most fishermen, I can remember pretty well where I got every fly (since to my shame I don't and can't tie my own), I could not remember this fly. But it *looks* right, and when I pick it up and hold it between my thumb and forefinger, it *feels* right as well.

I put it on. I begin to move my way down the pool, watching in the falling sunlight the fly disappearing under the surface, and when picked up looking entirely black, but when it made its arc, looking splendidly regal.

Suddenly, quite soon after I begin to fish, my line tightens, so automatically that it startles me, and in the twilight I have a salmon on.

"That's one," Peter said.

And we wait.

Down it goes, this majestic fish, and sulks and Peter watches from the beach, and then as if trying to make some assessment of me, it moves slowly upriver, pulling the line from my reel.

I reel until again I can feel the pressure. It was no grilse.

There is a moment when fighting a grilse a man or women will think they are in a fight—and I don't deny that they are. But this was a salmon, and the pressure on my rod, and on my arm, was seven times as great.

"David—come in, come in," Peter says, who could never stop his instruction or his teaching.

"It don't matter," I say, "because it's going to run."

And just then the salmon goes, and takes me with it, down almost out of the pool, zigging crazily from one side of the pool to the other, and then just as suddenly turning and coming back towards the rock, and jumping high in the air. Then it goes down and stays there. At this point I can feel the butt on my line.

The salmon was butting its head against the bottom, just beyond the rock, to loosen the fly's grip in its mouth. And then it comes up and jumps again.

"Well, they're still here," Peter says.

And down it goes again, this time out of the pool, and I run with it along the shore.

I have it hooked now about ten minutes.

The water is reddish and splendid in the darkening air, and I have no Polaroids on, and can't tell where exactly my fish is. Then it runs again. And my arm is aching. I'm not prepared and it almost straightens my rod out. Sensing it might have a chance at this it jumps high, a great fish, and comes down with the line sagging, and then tightening.

"Its got the leader tangled about its head," I say, noticing it moving sideways and butting its head once more. Then it runs again.

Now it is down, almost to the bend, and my backing, in a pocket between two rocks, and again it has taken to butting its head, to loosen my fly, and again an osprey flies high overhead, and again it is darkening.

I manage to wait on it, and reel my line in slowly, and follow it down.

Peter comes down with the net that was in the canoe most of the summer and hardly used, because so often we beach our fish. Now the salmon is taking small runs and stopping. My line moves over the water as if it is a slender magnet attached to some great being, going here and there, searching for a way out of something it does not understand.

I can't see it. But it is tiring, and coming to me now. And then suddenly it runs again, and I have to go into the water and follow it, as if I am on a slope in winter and trying to dig myself in.

Here it jumps, and starts to come back towards me, and I reel slowly, and then hold my rod crooked in my right arm again and back towards shore. After a few minutes I can see it, its tail moving slightly in the rapids, and Peter goes down below it, and comes up behind it.

"Here it is," he says.

After he nets it, he keeps it in the water.

"You don't have a camera do you?" he asks.

"No."

It is a great female filled with eggs. No wonder she fought so hard.

I held her by the tail and under the head, for five minutes or more, until I felt movement come back, and felt her get stronger in my grip, and I released her into the night, in a rip below

White Birch on the south branch of the Sevogle in late July of 1995, under an overhanging spruce tree, beside the flat red rock.

And we turned and walked back to the tent.

I thought of the salmon Richard Adams brought to my grandmother forty years before, and how I told her that some day I would travel along a river and hook a salmon as well. I did not know then that a Black Dose would make me think of that conversation forty years later, almost to the day, as I bit the fly off with my teeth and looked at its barb, still none the worse for wear. Then I remembered it was Dave Savage who had given me that fly one night long ago, before he travelled to the Restigouche.

And, too, it seemed only a moment had passed since Richard Adams had carried me down to his canoe where I sat in the stern for the picture that was later misplaced, and stared at the great train trestle and the silent, shadowed, and splendid green water.

"It's too bad we don't have a camera," Peter said. "An underwater camera," he said. "We'll have one when we go bone fishing in Florida."

The reason bone fishing attracted Peter was that it looked so esoteric and required patience, and you could see the tails of the fish, as they sulked about the large inlets. I knew he would be very good at bone fishing—or tuna fishing, or any other kind.

But I doubted if we'd ever get enough money to get there.

But maybe we would go fishing trout in Labrador, or over to the Restigouche again.

I changed into sweatpants, and cut up some onions and peeled some potatoes. The stove was going, and tea was brewing. We boiled the potatoes and the grilse in the same pot, and had the onions on a small pan next to the tea.

He told me a story, and I felt saddened by it. Gordon, my nemesis, and the golden boy of fishing, had taken to poaching, and had been caught, spearing fish in a pool with a speargun and a snorkel. He lost his truck and was fined. I never cared for Gordon. Still and all I felt sad about it. Felt sad for his father. Felt sad for the great river, and the fish. And yet it seemed to be as predictable in hindsight as anything else. It seemed as if this was what his look and his objections about me always seemed to signify—just as his trying to get the best deal in trading his hockey and baseball cards did.

Then it got dark enough not to see anything. The trees behind us, the water in front of us, were unified in blackness. And then the stars came out, thousands of them.

It was now 1995. My brothers and I were building another camp, on a hill, beyond those very darkened trees by about eight miles. It stood as a testament to my brother John's great love of the woods, though he didn't fish and rarely hunted, and his love of canoeing. And it stood as a testament to my love of those same woods, and our family of brothers who never had a camp as children. And it stood also as testament that I would come back to fish again, no matter where I travelled or where I lived. For it was *here* where I lived. It was here where I wrote, and thought of how complete and uncomplicated life was meant to be.

So our camp, which was in the process of being built that summer, was the guardian of all of that. Its roof was angled, its shadows warm, while our camp log brought over from our first camp lay on the table.

I hoped to travel the whole river the next summer. I hoped. I was born without great physical ability, yet I had tested the physical life in the best way I could. I had tested it now for twenty years. This river I had walked a dozen times, and had taken fish in almost every pool. I had done after a fashion, filled with as many false starts and failures as one could imagine, what I had set out to do. And I turned it into my art and wrote about it in one way or another my entire life. This is not a great accomplishment by any means, but it is an accomplishment for me. So then I had told my grandmother the truth that day. I had resurrected from my past life of much uncertainty and clumsiness the fish that I stared at in my grandmother's kitchen when I was four years old. Perhaps my grandmother knew this. Perhaps she too was watching. Perhaps I remembered that night, or a little later, that that fly, the Black Dose, was given to me by David Savage.

We heard a splash as a deer crossed the river and went up into the hills just below us, near where I had released the salmon, and towards the place Peter had fallen on the bear when he was not much older than his oldest girl is now.

I took out my after-dinner close-to-bedtime chew of plug and put it in, and had a spit as Peter lighted a cigarette. And then I knew it was time to tell the story.

"Once at an old camp," I began, "a friend of ours came in for a fish. He was a Mr. Simms, and this was a long, long time ago. He had owned the camp when he was young and had built the camp too, but when he went away his cousins had taken it from him. Stole it really and were even proud of the fact that he didn't complain too much.

"Now that he was back they told him he could fish if he wanted but he could not be a partner or make any claim to it. Mr. Simms who had owned this camp and had built it as well thought that this was rather cold of them.

"So they went down the river in a canoe and all the way into the narrows, and all got fish except him, who was a very wise friend and a very good and quite patient fisherman. But he had no luck that day. And so they all teased him.

" 'You can't fish,' they said, 'so what do you need a camp for?'

"And he told them he was using a wonderful little fly the name of I don't remember. And that he would get the fish he really wanted, the fish everyone was looking for. It was a fly called Patience and Perseverance and Integrity.

"So the four of them went back to the camp, and they sat up late at night and played cards and drank, and talked about how wonderful their camp was, and said they wished Mr. Simms had made this certain part different or that a little different, or one angle wasn't quite right, or it wasn't flush in just one place. And he sat there very patiently and listened as they complained about his handiwork.

" 'We should get you to rebuild it,' they said.

"And just before they went to bed he said he had to leave, and he added, as an afterthought, and as if he was just remembering it, that he had hidden a quart of Black Diamond rum in the camp when he was young, the year he had built it. But that he couldn't exactly remember where."

I stopped speaking and had a spit and Peter looked at me.

"Now he didn't get into the camp until a week went by, for he was a walking boss who had to go from camp to camp. And he decided to visit his cousins. For his cousins were hard pressed to get out of the woods, having to cut pulp every day. And when he went to the camp—well, you know how it looked."

"No," Peter said.

"Well, it looked as if it had disappeared. It was the strangest sight. In fact, you could stare right through the camp and not see a camp at all, except for one opened window, with the glass broken.

"There was a huge pile where the camp used to be. A door, a shingle, a beam—here and there a dish towel and a cup. Even the outhouse had been turned on its side, and the contents searched.

"And the cousins? Well they were a sorrowful sight. And they didn't even notice him. And they were all still fighting amongst themselves, and blaming each other, with black eyes and pulled hair, and suspiciously searching each other, and rolling about in the dirt, and the canoe had a hole in it.

"None of them could find that rum. And even until late in life they believed it was there.

"You could say that they had gone right down to their backing trying to find it. There was a big hole in the earth, where that camp had been—oh, they had dug about eight feet.

"Well, my friend, the great Mr. Simms got the fish he wanted, for soon, fighting amongst themselves, they left him in peace, and he rebuilt the camp, and except for a few angles it was exactly the way it had been, and he toasted them all with a drink of rum that he had gone to the liquor store to buy."

"I see," Peter said.

"And that's how it is when you are fishers of men," I said, remembering Mr. Simms and his twin brother and smiling.

"David."

"What?"

"Don't let anyone else hear you talking like that. I can take it—because I know you."

"Well," I said, finishing my tea, "tomorrow is another day—"

"Tomorrow we'll get fish," Peter said, "I guarantee it. Remember that small pool—when we came in to the South Branch from the other side—walked up from the Narrows Pool and—"

And then all sounds became unified with the river, and the fire, and the fly dope kept the bugs away.

The fish move easily in this clear flowing water that is constantly moving against the direction they are going. The male turns right or left past shallows, past boulders, always searching for the channel.

They move into one of the great hidden tributaries, while others skirt towards some unknown destination. In mid-morning they come to a small falls, and rest beneath it.

They have come home. Swimming in water running fresh and clean, they feel the sun's energy; and come for the first time, the first time ever, into the realm of lines on the water.

About the Author

DAVID ADAMS RICHARDS is best known for his Miramichi trilogy: *Nights Below Station Street* (1988), winner of the Governor General's Award; *Evening Snow Will Bring Such Peace* (1990), winner of the Canadian Authors Association Award; and *For Those Who Hunt the Wounded Down* (1993). His recent work of non-fiction, *Hockey Dreams,* was a national bestseller. He lives with his family in Toronto.